British Railways
The First 25 Years

Volume 5
The South West
North Devon, Plymouth
and Cornwall

The joint Plymouth Railway Circle and RCTS 'Exmoor Ranger' five-coach rail tour visited a number of lines that were due to lose their passenger service on 27th March 1965, and also the Halwill to Petrockstow section which had been closed to all traffic four weeks prior to this tour. Ivatt Class '2' 2-6-2Ts No's 41206 and 41291 are heading the train at Barnstaple. On shed is Collett '2251' 0-6-0 No. 3205, allocated to Exmouth Junction, which will bank the train from Braunton to Mortehoe, before taking over for the return from Ilfracombe to Barnstaple and on to Exeter via Dulverton and Taunton. No. 3205 would be withdrawn shortly afterwards, but was saved for preservation, the only one of its class to survive.

BRITISH RAILWAYS

The First 25 Years

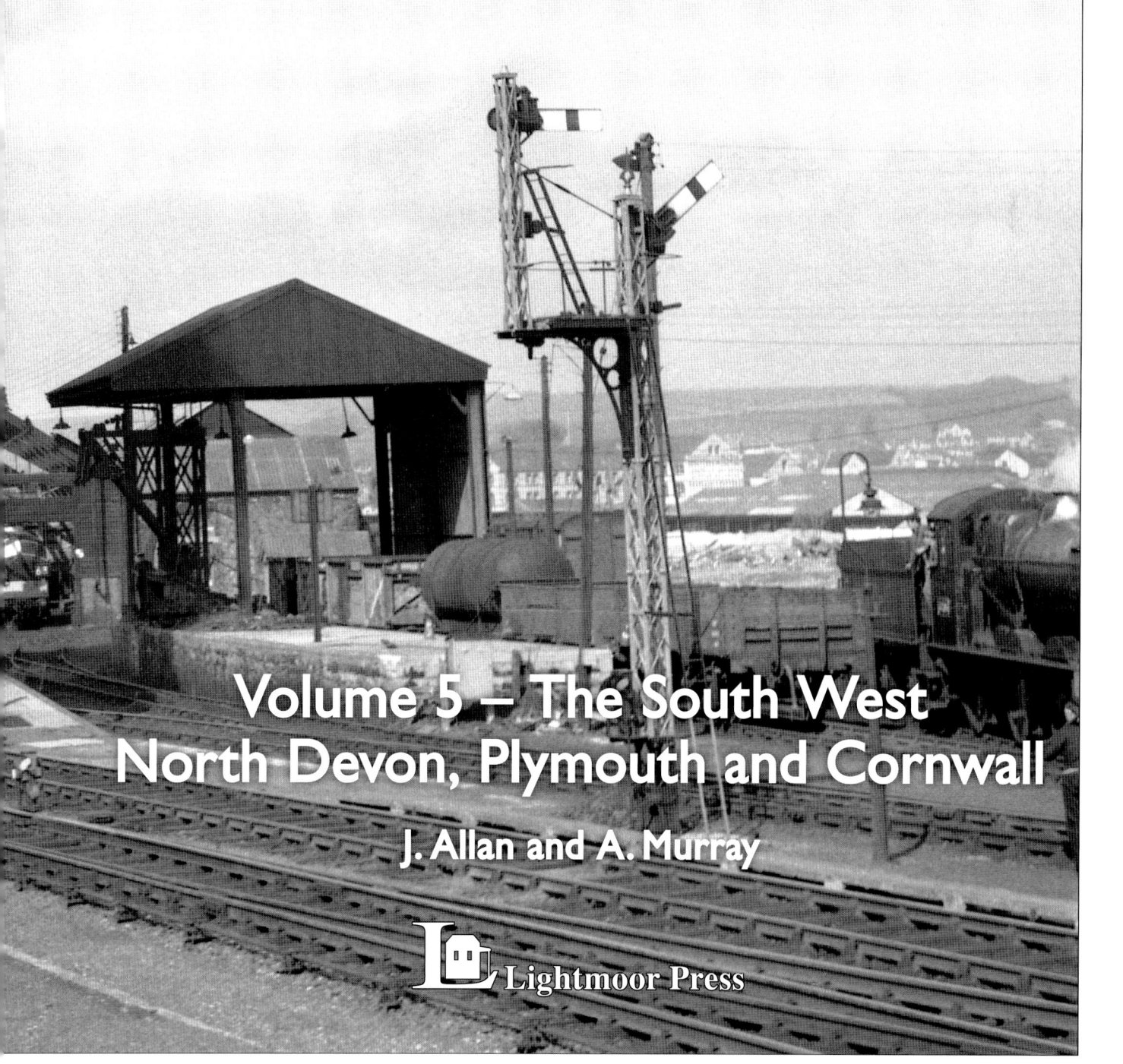

Volume 5 – The South West
North Devon, Plymouth and Cornwall

J. Allan and A. Murray

Lightmoor Press

Cover photographs

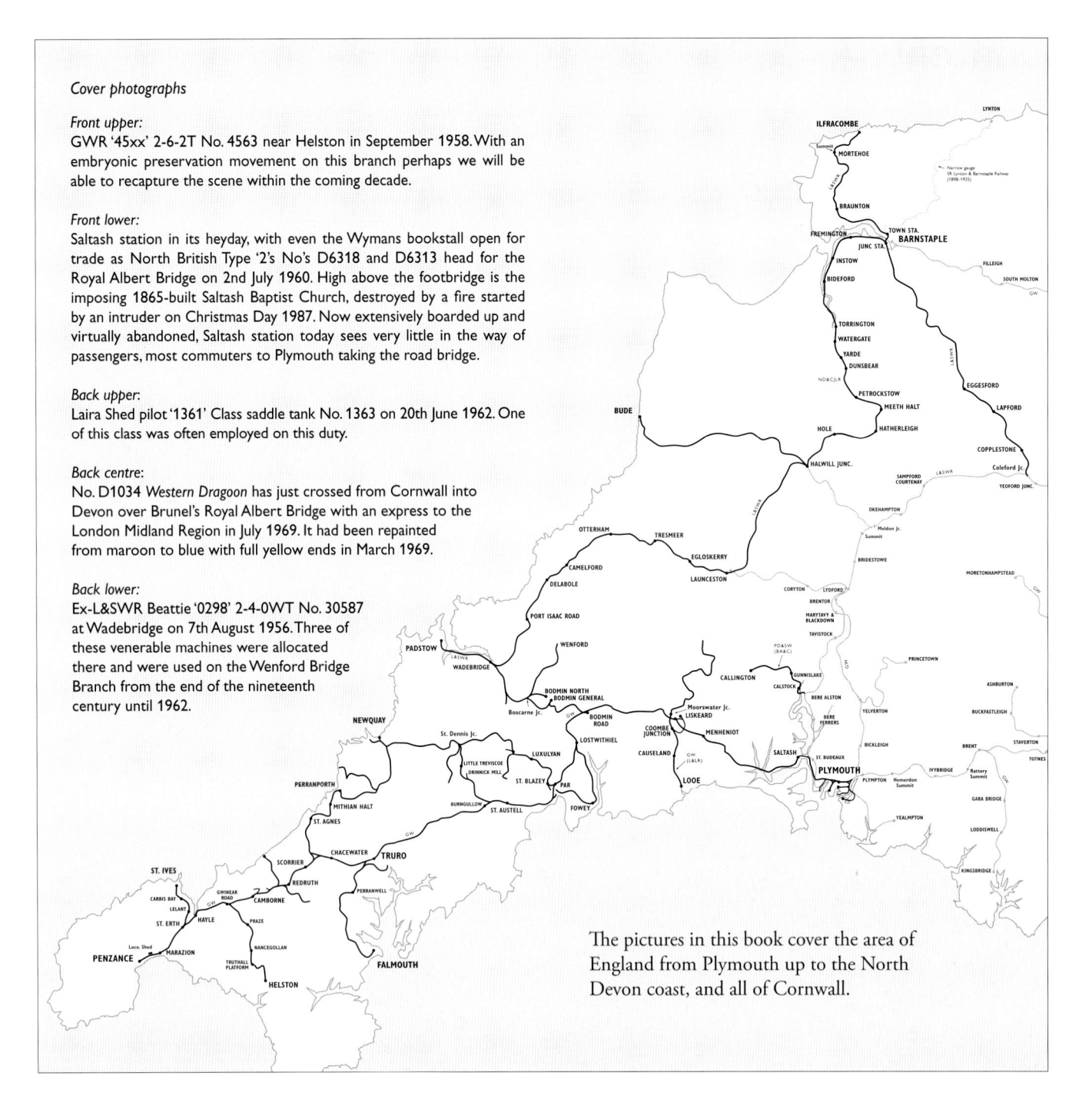

Front upper:
GWR '45xx' 2-6-2T No. 4563 near Helston in September 1958. With an embryonic preservation movement on this branch perhaps we will be able to recapture the scene within the coming decade.

Front lower:
Saltash station in its heyday, with even the Wymans bookstall open for trade as North British Type '2's No's D6318 and D6313 head for the Royal Albert Bridge on 2nd July 1960. High above the footbridge is the imposing 1865-built Saltash Baptist Church, destroyed by a fire started by an intruder on Christmas Day 1987. Now extensively boarded up and virtually abandoned, Saltash station today sees very little in the way of passengers, most commuters to Plymouth taking the road bridge.

Back upper:
Laira Shed pilot '1361' Class saddle tank No. 1363 on 20th June 1962. One of this class was often employed on this duty.

Back centre:
No. D1034 *Western Dragoon* has just crossed from Cornwall into Devon over Brunel's Royal Albert Bridge with an express to the London Midland Region in July 1969. It had been repainted from maroon to blue with full yellow ends in March 1969.

Back lower:
Ex-L&SWR Beattie '0298' 2-4-0WT No. 30587 at Wadebridge on 7th August 1956. Three of these venerable machines were allocated there and were used on the Wenford Bridge Branch from the end of the nineteenth century until 1962.

The pictures in this book cover the area of England from Plymouth up to the North Devon coast, and all of Cornwall.

© Lightmoor Press, J. Allan, A. Murray, 2016. Reprinted 2023.
Designed by Stephen Phillips.

British Library Cataloguing-in-Publication Data.
A catalogue record for this book is available from the British Library.
ISBN 9781911038146

All rights reserved. No part of this publication may be reproduced, stored in a retrieval system or transmitted in any form or by any means, electronic, mechanical, photocopying, recording or otherwise, without the written permission of the publisher.

LIGHTMOOR PRESS
Unit 144B, Lydney Trading Estate, Harbour Road, Lydney, Gloucestershire GL15 5EJ
www.lightmoor.co.uk

Lightmoor Press is an imprint of Black Dwarf Lightmoor Publications Ltd.

Printed in Poland www.lfbookservices.co.uk

Contents

	Introduction and Acknowledgements	6
1	**Southern Region – North Devon**	**7**
	Coleford Junction to Barnstaple	7
	Barnstaple Junction	8
	Ilfracombe	17
	Barnstaple to Torrington	23
	Bideford	23
	Torrington	25
	Torrington to Halwill Junction	28
	Halwill Junction	35
2	**Plymouth**	**38**
	North Road	38
	Laira	64
	Friary	74
	Keyham	77
	Millbay Docks	78
3	**Southern Region – Cornwall**	**80**
	Callington	80
	Bude	84
	Halwill Junction to Padstow	86
	Otterham	87
	Wadebridge	88
	Wadebridge to Padstow	95
	Bodmin to Wadebridge	97
	Bodmin North	100
	The Beattie well tanks and the Wenford Bridge Branch	101
4	**Western Region main line – Plymouth to Penzance**	**106**
	The Royal Albert Bridge and Saltash	106
	Menheniot	114
	Liskeard	115
	Moorswater	115
	Bodmin Road	116
	Lostwithiel	118
	Par	120
	St. Austell	121
	Truro	123
	Scorrier	131
	Redruth	132
	Camborne	133
	Gwinear Road	135
	Hayle	138
	St. Erth	139
	Marazion	143
	Penzance	145
5	**Western Region – Cornish branch lines**	**156**
	Looe	156
	Bodmin Road to Wadebridge	161
	Fowey	164
	Parkandillack	172
	The Newquay Branches	174
	Falmouth	179
	Helston	182
	St. Ives	186

North British-built 'Warship' No. D835 *Pegasus* crosses from Devon into Cornwall over Brunel's iconic Royal Albert Bridge at Saltash with the 3.46pm Plymouth-Penzance all stations service on 24th June 1963. The train eventually arrived in Penzance at 6.59pm, the 79½ miles taking almost 3¼ hours!

Introduction and Acknowledgements

This is the fifth in a series of books, depicting the first 25 years of British Railways, which will eventually cover the whole of Great Britain. As we have said previously, we have been fortunate to have had access to hundreds of different pictures from which to choose the final selection presented here. We have included photographs spanning the early British Railways era through to the pre-TOPS diesels, although the emphasis is on that interesting transitional period of the late 1950s and early 1960s.

This volume covers the South West of England from Plymouth westwards into Cornwall, and follows on from Volume 4, which dealt primarily with the lines in Devon. We have included here the North Devon lines of the Southern Region which had much in common with their Cornish counterparts. There was heavy seasonal holiday traffic on Summer Saturdays and Bank Holidays, while on weekdays everything was less hectic and more peaceful, especially on the branch lines serving the rural communities. There was also a lack of heavy industry, with the exception of the dockyards and china clay. The railway history of this area is complex with many short-lived companies, mergers, running powers, light railways, etc and we have not tried to unravel the detail of these, choosing to leave this to specialist 'line' histories.

We have attempted to produce a mix which we hope everyone will like, from bucolic branch lines clinging to economic survival through to the distinctive Cornish main line of the Western Region, not forgetting the strange semi-industrial lines serving the high volume and environmentally destructive china clay industry, through what had previously been a rural landscape. Operations centred on Plymouth where both Southern and Western Regions had large sheds. It is also worth noting the level of operational co-operation dating back to the rival pre-grouping companies: access to the former London & South Western Railway's Plymouth Friary station was via running rights through the Great Western Railway's North Road station.

Both dieselisation and rationalisation came early to the area; the Southern Region lines were transferred to the Western Region in January 1963 and severely cut-back by the end of the following year. When pannier tank No. 1369 was sold for preservation in November 1964 it was the last British Railways' steam locomotive west of Exeter, and Doctor Beeching's axe had already hit the Western's branches hard. However, the dieselisation had a character all to itself, with the Western Region's adoption of hydraulic transmission a short-lived last stand by Swindon which was ultimately swept away in the standardisation drive of the late 1960s and early 1970s. The far South West was home to the five heavyweight North British 'D600' Type '4's and over half of the smaller Type '2' 'D6300's.

We have arranged the pictures as in previous volumes, combining geography with 'time travel' to produce what we think is an interesting and reasonably logical ordering of the material. We have included a separate chapter on Plymouth, with trips around the motive power depots of both Western and Southern Regions, and have devoted a number of pages to the Beattie well tanks on the Wenford Bridge Branch. 'Castles', 'Counties', '14xx' and 'Prairies' contrast with Bulleid Pacifics and 'M7's, while the ubiquitous 'N' Class were joined by an influx of LM&SR designed 2-6-2Ts for the final years of steam on the Southern.

Acknowledgements

Most of the pictures in this volume are from the *www.Rail-Online.co.uk* collection, with contributions from photographers Peter Kerslake and Robert Darlaston who each took many excellent pictures in the area during the 1950s and early 1960s, and supplemented by a few photographs from the Lens of Sutton Association collection. We have included many full page portraits which bring out the quality of the photographs taken all those years ago.

Our thanks go to Robert Darlaston, Maurice Dart, Peter Kerslake and Martin Street for their help with the captions, and our old friend Vic Smith for helping identify many of the locations. Any errors remaining are of course entirely the responsibility of the authors and publishers.

References

We have consulted a number of books to provide details of locomotives and workings and in particular, the RCTS Great Western Railway and BR Standard locomotive histories and the appropriate R.A. Cooke *Track layout Diagrams*. The Irwell Press *Main Line to the West of England* series, *The North Devon Line*, *An Illustrated History of Exmoor's Railways* and *An Illustrated History of the North Cornwall Railway* have been particularly useful, as were their *Book of...* series on Great Western and Southern Railway classes.

J Allan and A Murray 2016

1 – Southern Region – North Devon

The route from Crediton to Barnstaple was built by the Taw Vale Extension and Dock Company, opening as a broad gauge line in 1854. It had gained Parliamentary approval in 1845 and was then caught up in the 'Gauge Wars' and the financial crash after the 'Railway Mania' of 1845-7. The Taw Vale company changed its name to the North Devon Railway and Dock Company in 1851; the London & South Western Railway leased the line in 1862 and converted it to mixed gauge before formally taking it over in 1865. An extension from Barnstaple to Bideford was opened in 1872, but Ilfracombe was not reached until 1874 because of fierce debate over the route to be chosen.

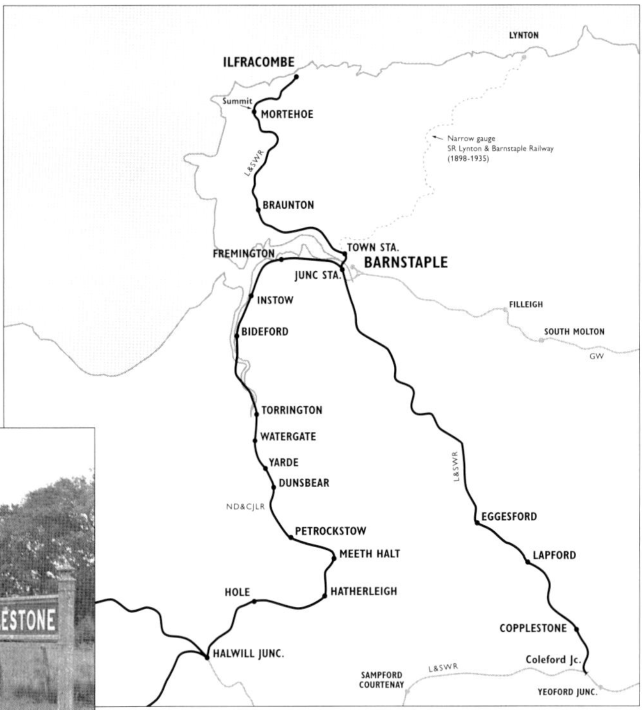

Coleford Junction to Barnstaple

'Warship' No. D868 *Zephyr* on an Exeter-bound train in 1966/7 at Copplestone with the crew about to hand over the single line tablet. This was the first point on the North Devon line where the drivers had to collect a single line token. The signal box, built on a stone base, closed in October 1971.

Ex-L&SWR Drummond '700' Class 0-6-0 No. 30315 at Lapford on 11th June 1956. The 'Ambrosia Ltd Dried Milk Works' on the right of the picture employed several hundred people and generated much traffic for the line. Lapford station was cut in two by the road bridge carrying the A377 road across the line at an angle, as can be seen in the background; the station had one platform on either side of the bridge, each with its own booking office.

'Battle of Britain' 4-6-2 No. 34066 *Spitfire* arriving at Lapford with a train from Barnstaple in the early 1960s, following its transfer from Stewarts Lane to Exmouth Junction in February 1961. This picture was taken from below the A377 road bridge.
Lens of Sutton Association

Barnstaple Junction

Barnstaple Junction was the title of the station between 1874 and 1970, reverting to plain Barnstaple thereafter, following the demise of the Ilfracombe line.

No. 30315 is seen again, arriving at Barnstaple Junction with a local freight on 13th June 1956. It had been allocated to Exmouth Junction since late 1954 but moved away to Salisbury in early 1958.

'West Country' 4-6-2 No. 34016 *Bodmin* departs from Barnstaple Junction with the 6.25am Yeovil Town to Ilfracombe, also on 13th June. No. 34016 went new to Exmouth Junction in November 1945 as No. 21C116 and was renumbered in July 1948. It was transferred to Ramsgate in February 1958 when it went into Eastleigh Works to be rebuilt. *Bodmin* was one of no less than eighteen 'Light Pacifics' bought for preservation after languishing at Woodham Brothers' scrapyard in Barry, South Wales.

An 'M7' 0-4-4T arriving at Barnstaple Junction with the Torrington portion of the 'Atlantic Coast Express' on 13th June 1956. The sharply curved, check-railed line over the Taw Bridge to Barnstaple Town and on to Ilfracombe is on the right of the picture.

'N' Class 2-6-0 No. 31856 was one of five additional 'N' Class engines transferred to Exmouth Junction in January 1961 to supplement the extensive fleet already based there. The train is unusual as it includes eight identical SR open mineral wagons all running together, so this may have been a special consignment of some type.

No. 34035 *Shaftesbury* arrives in Platform 2 at Barnstaple Junction. This was the only part of the country where Pacifics regularly worked tender-first on either passenger or freight duties. No. 34035 was transferred to Exmouth Junction in January 1958 from Plymouth Friary where it had been allocated since late 1950; it was withdrawn in June 1963.

Another tender-first Pacific, No. 34066 *Spitfire* with plenty of steam to spare as it waits further down Platform 2. No. 34066 kept its original 4,500 gallon tender until withdrawn and the picture shows how the 'raves' were cut away in 1958 to improve access for the crew. The headcode discs indicate this is a train to Torrington.

Another shot of No. 34066 *Spitfire*, this time from the footbridge. There is lots of activity with another Bulleid Pacific marshalling its train in Platform 1 on the left, and a third just visible on the right in Platform 3 under the canopy. No. 34066 spent its early years in the South East at Ramsgate, and then Stewarts Lane, before moving to Exmouth Junction in February 1961. It left for Salisbury in September 1964 and was withdrawn in September 1966.

Ivatt 2-6-2T No. 41298 in Platform 2 with a Torrington train on 11th November 1962. Built at Crewe in October 1951 for the Southern Region, it moved from its first shed at Bricklayers Arms to Barnstaple Junction in 1953. No. 41298 left ten years later, to Weymouth and then, in October 1966, to Nine Elms. In 1967 it was purchased directly from British Railways by the Ivatt Locomotive Trust, going to the Longmoor Military Railway. After this closed No. 41298 moved to Quainton Road in December 1970 and a heavy overhaul commenced. In 2008, No. 41298 was relocated to the Isle of Wight, arriving at Havenstreet on 28th November.

Another 2-6-2T, No. 41216, departs to Torrington on 18th July 1963. It was one of the second batch turned out from Crewe Works in September 1948 and was originally equipped with a vacuum controlled regulator for push-pull working. The former London Midland Region engine was transferred to Plymouth Friary in late 1961 and moved to Barnstaple Junction in January 1963. No. 41216 stayed there until November 1964 when it moved to Exmouth Junction.

'West Country' No. 34002 *Salisbury* comes off the Torrington line with a freight working, which has an insulated fish van as the second wagon, on 23rd August 1963. It had been at Exmouth Junction from new in June 1945 and only left when that shed lost all its Pacifics in September 1964. In the background is the start of the reverse curve to Ilfracombe and in front of that is the stock yard of the Devon Concrete Works.

Ten surplus ex-London Brighton & South Coast Railway Stroudley 'E1' 0-6-0Ts were rebuilt to 'E1R' 0-6-2Ts in the late-1920s, each with a radial trailing axle, extended rear bunker/water tank and a rounded cab roof for use on the North Devon & Cornwall Junction Light Railway (ND&CJLR) line between Torrington and Halwill Junction. Newly renumbered No. 32696 (originally LB&SCR No. 104 *Brittany* of 1876), with Southern Railway-style British Railways number, was on shed with classmates at Barnstaple Junction in 1948/9. It had been rebuilt from an 'E1' in December 1928 and lasted until January 1956, having received BR lined black paintwork in September 1950. The shed was not equipped with a wheel drop but was provided with this sophisticated hoist, running on its own pair of rails. It could move along the length of more than one engine, allowing two engines to have their wheels removed at any one time. Whether this was ever necessary is not recorded. *Lens of Sutton Association*

Two 'M7' 0-4-4Ts, No's 30247 and 30251, at Barnstaple Junction Shed in the early 1960s. Both engines were 'M7/1's with short frames and front sandboxes on the splashers, and were built at the L&SWR Nine Elms works in 1897. No. 30247 had been at Barnstaple Junction since 1937, apart from a couple of months at Nine Elms in late 1952 and was withdrawn there in October 1961; No. 30251 had been transferred from Bournemouth in March 1951 but moved to Feltham in January 1963, six months before withdrawal. The shed had seven 'M7's in 1959 and they were used on shunting and local work including the Barnstaple to Torrington line, although they did not run over the severely restricted ND&CJLR from there to Halwill. Not all tank wagons in the area carried milk; those in this photograph are petrol tanks.

'N' Class 2-6-0 No. 31839 at Barnstaple Junction Shed with 'M7' 0-4-4T No. 30025 on 22nd June 1962. No. 31839 was one of the twenty consecutively numbered engines, No's 31830-31849, at Exmouth Junction during the 1950s and into the early 1960s; it was withdrawn there at the end of 1963. No. 30025 had been at Exmouth Junction since Southern Railway days; it was withdrawn in May 1964. The original shed is on the right with its arched entrance bricked up and used for workshops and offices, and on the left is the wooden shed built when the standard gauge line reached the town in the 1860s. It was the main depot in North Devon with sub-sheds at Ilfracombe and Torrington, and at one time employed over a hundred men.

'Battle of Britain' No. 34081 *92 Squadron* with steam up and ready to move off shed, probably in 1964. It had been transferred to Exmouth Junction in October 1957 and left in July 1964 for Eastleigh. In its final days the shed became increasingly decrepit and closed in August 1964, although diesels continued to stable there in 1965. The roof had been badly damaged but the wooden beams had been left in place.

No. 34019 *Bideford* crossing the Taw with an Up train on 26th August 1950. Built in December 1945 as No. 21C119, it was renumbered in May 1948. It went new to Exmouth Junction but left for a few months in 1948, returning at the end of that year. *Bideford*'s stay was brief – it was transferred to Nine Elms in April 1951 and never came back to the West Country shed.

An unidentified 'Light' Pacific crossing the River Taw with a train from Ilfracombe on 11th June 1956. From the end of the Junction station platform the line followed a long reverse 'S', check-railed and with a 15mph speed limit throughout, right to Barnstaple Town station. The second half of the curve was over the 200 yards-long wrought iron bridge which had fifteen pairs of girders, each forty feet long.

Collett '2251' 0-6-0 No. 3205 crosses the Taw Bridge with the 'The Exmoor Ranger' railtour, which was organised jointly by the Plymouth Railway Circle and the RCTS, on 27th March 1965. No. 3205 was working the train from Ilfracombe to Barnstaple and then on to Exeter via Dulverton and Taunton. Note the check-rail on the tight curve.

'Warship' No. D806 *Cambrian* crossing the Taw Bridge with a ten-coach train from Ilfracombe, probably on a summer Saturday in 1967. The hydraulics took over the passenger workings on the former Southern Railway lines from September 1964. No. D806 was repainted in maroon with small yellow warning panels in June 1966 and received full yellow ends in January 1968. As can be seen in the foreground, the bridge was No. 3 and the tightness of the curve and the check-rail are clearly visible.

Another Pacific approaching Barnstaple Town station from Ilfracombe. The rear coaches are on the Pottington Swing Bridge over the River Yeo where it joins the estuary of the River Taw. The 59ft long iron bridge was controlled by the Pottington signal box visible in the centre background.

Returning shoppers and holidaymakers wait as Exmouth Junction 'N' Class 2-6-0 No. 31830 arrives at Barnstaple Town with the 5.15 pm Barnstaple Junction to Ilfracombe train on 16th June 1961. The disused bay platform on the left was formerly used by the 1ft 11½in. narrow gauge line to Lynton & Lynmouth, which closed in September 1935. Barnstaple Town station was built by the L&SWR for the 1898 opening of the Lynton line, replacing an earlier station built nearer to the river bridge. The canopy was cut back following the closure of the Lynton line. *Robert Darlaston*

Ilfracombe

The line from Barnstaple to Ilfracombe was projected from around 1854 and authorised in 1864, but much controversy over the proposed route delayed the start of construction until 1871. The Barnstaple & Ilfracombe Railway was finally opened in 1874 at which date it was acquired by the London & South Western Railway. Rationalisation of services and the infrastructure began after the Western Region took over responsibility for the line in January 1963, but the inevitable was only delayed and the line closed in October 1970.

No. 34004 *Yeovil* about to drop down the 1 in 36 gradient into Ilfracombe station with the 'Devon Belle' on 1st September 1950. An Exmouth Junction engine from new in June 1945, this was the 'Light Pacific' best-known for its exploits in the 1948 Interchange Trials on the Highland main line in Scotland. It had been given a wedge-shaped cab in early 1948 and had been repainted in BR green livery during a General overhaul completed in April 1950. The line from Barnstaple was originally single track but was doubled in 1891, apart from the short section over the River Taw bridge at Barnstaple. It was singled again in 1967 in an attempt to reduce costs but the last passenger train ran on 3rd October 1970. Subsequently the track was left in situ as an embryonic preservation attempt failed, and although an inspection train ventured to Ilfracombe on 26 February 1975, track lifting commenced in June of that year.

Viewed from a train hauled by an 'N' Class 2-6-0, a 'West Country' climbs up the 1 in 36 out of Ilfracombe with three coaches and three vans on 14th June 1956. Here, the line ran along the side of the Slade valley and, after the train emerged from the Slade Tunnel, gave arriving passengers their first glimpse of the sea.

An unidentified 'Light Pacific' has completed the climb out of Ilfracombe and is approaching Slade Tunnel with an Up train on 11th June 1956. The twin bores were each 69 yards long and the Up one was the original from 1874, the Down being added in 1891 when the line was doubled.

Ilfracombe station was situated high above the town as photographed from the top of Torrs Walk on 15th June 1956. It was built up on extensive earthworks and was 225 feet above sea level, necessitating a long walk down a steep slope into the town. The engine shed is at the right-hand side and the station is in the centre with several rakes of coaches stored in the carriage sidings in front.

No. 34110 66 Squadron departs from Ilfracombe with a two-coach train on 6th May 1961. It was the last 'Light Pacific 'built, emerging from Brighton Works in January 1951. No. 34110 went new to Bournemouth, moving to Exmouth Junction in March 1959 and was withdrawn from there in November 1963. The 65ft turntable was installed in 1925 to enable 'N' Class 2-6-0s to work Exeter-Ilfracombe services, and until 1947 it was the only Southern Railway turntable west of Exeter which could handle a Bulleid Pacific. The engine shed was rebuilt in 1929, using concrete blocks from the Exmouth Junction concrete works, as part of a major improvement programme at Ilfracombe which included longer platforms and additional siding space.

Although strictly just outside our time frame, we could not resist using these two pictures of Bulleid 'West Country' No. 21C117 *Ilfracombe* at Ilfracombe taken on 20th June 1947 with the inaugural 'Devon Belle'. No. 21C117 entered service at Exmouth Junction in December 1945 and its malachite green paintwork with yellow horizontal lining stripes has clearly been 'bulled-up' for the occasion; it was renumbered as No. 34017 in May 1948 and was modified with a wedge-fronted cab in late 1953. The 'Devon Belle' utilised spare coaches owned by the Pullman Company and ran on Fridays, Saturdays, Sundays and Mondays for the summer season up to the end of October. The 'Light Pacific' only worked the train as far as Wilton where a 'Merchant Navy' took over to Waterloo. Patronage declined after the 1949 season and the service was reduced, and eventually ceased in September 1954.

CHAPTER 1 - SOUTHERN REGION - NORTH DEVON

'West Country' No. 34013 *Okehampton* ready for departure in the mid-1950s. It acquired the wedge-fronted cab in May 1954 and was rebuilt in late-1957. No. 34013 went new to Exmouth Junction in October 1945, moved to Plymouth Friary in April 1948 and back to Exmouth Junction in May 1951; after rebuilding it went to Bricklayers Arms.

Passengers walk to their train that has arrived at Ilfracombe behind maroon-liveried 'Warship' No. D806 *Cambrian* in the summer of 1968.

No. D806 *Cambrian* has run around its train, coupled on, and now waits to depart from Ilfracombe. The 'Warship' was repainted in maroon in June 1966 and received the full yellow ends in January 1968, retaining this livery until March 1971.

The view up the hill out of the station. No. D806 *Cambrian* ready for the climb up the 1 in 36 gradient to Mortehoe from a standing start, but with only four coaches this should not trouble the 2,200 bhp Type '4' diesel-hydraulic.

Barnstaple to Torrington

The L&SWR gained Parliamentary approval to extend its North Devon line five miles up the Torridge Valley from Bideford to Torrington in 1865, but then attempted to abandon the extension because of the prohibitive engineering costs involved. However, it suffered a legal defeat and was forced to build the line, although construction did not begin until 1870 and the opening was not for a further two years. The passenger service to Barnstaple was withdrawn in October 1965, the line remaining open for freight until officially closed in 1982.

Ivatt 2-6-2T No. 41283 heads towards Fremington from Barnstaple on a Torrington train which is returning an empty milk tanker to the loading point there. In this view taken from Sticklepath bridge, the Up main siding and headshunt are on the right with the gate to the private siding of the Devon Concrete Works.

Bideford

Barnstaple Junction-allocated 'M7' No. 30255 stands at Bideford sometime in the 1950s. Built at Nine Elms in 1897, it was withdrawn from 72E in September 1960 after spending the last nine years of its working life there.
Lens of Sutton Association

Ivatt 2-6-2T No. 41316 making its way northwards from Bideford station with a train from Torrington to Barnstaple. No. 41316 was at Barnstaple Junction between September 1963 and June 1964 when it was transferred to Nine Elms. The stretch of line from Bideford to Torrington was expensive to build because it ran literally through the gardens of properties backing onto the railway at Bideford. Just visible in the background is the roofline of the 'Royal Hotel' which was so close to the line it built an entrance from its second floor onto the Up platform.

Torrington

Another Barnstaple Junction (72E) 'M7', No. 30251, stands at Torrington with a train for Barnstaple Junction in the early 1960s. It was allocated to 72E from March 1951 until leaving for Feltham in January 1963. It would not last long there, being withdrawn from Eastleigh in July the same year.

'M7' 0-4-4T No. 30250 after arrival at Torrington from Barnstaple Junction in the mid-1950s. It was allocated there from 1931 until withdrawn in August 1957. The first vehicle is an ex-LM&SR bogie brake, followed by two ex-L&SWR coaches, a corridor brake composite and a non-corridor carriage on a Southern Railway underframe. No. 30250 was an 'M7/1' with short frames and front sandboxes on the splasher; it is in the second version of BR lined black with the cream and grey line following the full extent of the splasher and sandbox.   *Lens of Sutton Association*

There is plenty of activity at Torrington in July 1964 as No. 41216 is about to leave with a short freight and a classmate is shunting the stock for its next working. The 2-6-2T was transferred from Plymouth Friary to Barnstaple Junction in January 1963 and stayed until November 1964 when it moved to Exmouth Junction. In 1959 Barnstaple had five of these 2-6-2Ts and two or three were normally based at Torrington, until the shed there closed, to work over the former North Devon & Cornwall Junction Light Railway and also on passenger and freight duties to Barnstaple.

An unidentified 2-6-2T with a mixed train at Torrington in August 1964. A single coach was attached at Petrockstow to the afternoon freight from Halwill Junction to convey the returning workers who travelled each day to work at Marland clay works. The gantry over the siding where the milk tanker is standing, carried pipes used to load milk from lorries into the rail tanks. New loading facilities were erected on the Up platform in 1975, but the traffic ceased in 1978.

On the same day, No. 41248 is ready for departure to Barnstaple with two coaches and a milk tanker. It was one of the British Railways-built '2MT' tanks and was only at Barnstaple Junction for its last few months in service. It arrived there from Bristol Barrow Road at the end of 1963 and was withdrawn in September 1964 when the shed closed.

CHAPTER 1 - SOUTHERN REGION - NORTH DEVON

North British Type '2' diesel-hydraulic No. D6337 in the late 1960s arriving at Torrington off the ND&CJLR with a short train of loaded china clay wagons from Marland and Meeth bound for Fowey Docks. Weeds are already beginning to take hold in the ballast, in complete contrast to the earlier pictures. However, the line between Barnstaple and Meeth survived because of the clay traffic until August 1982. No. D6337 itself lasted until October 1971, the freight services on the line being taken over by Class '25' diesel-electrics transferred from the London Midland Region.

Torrington to Halwill Junction

The twenty mile long North Devon and Cornwall Junction Light Railway (ND&CJLR) from Torrington to Halwill Junction opened in July 1923. It had been granted a Light Railway Order in 1914, but the First World War intervened and construction did not begin until June 1922. The line was worked for its first three decades by 'E1R' 0-6-2Ts which had been rebuilt from ex-LB&SCR Stroudley 'E1' 0-6-0Ts by adding a radial trailing axle and larger bunker. They were replaced by Ivatt 2-6-2Ts which first arrived at Barnstaple Junction Shed in May 1953 and had completely taken over by 1957. ND&CJLR passenger services were withdrawn on 1st March 1965 and the line between Meeth and Halwill Junction was closed.

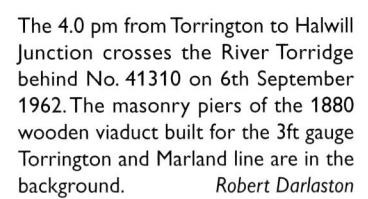

The 4.0 pm from Torrington to Halwill Junction crosses the River Torridge behind No. 41310 on 6th September 1962. The masonry piers of the 1880 wooden viaduct built for the 3ft gauge Torrington and Marland line are in the background. *Robert Darlaston*

Ivatt 2-6-2T No. 41310 pulls into Watergate Halt with the 4.0 pm Torrington to Halwill Junction on 3rd September 1962. The platform, fencing and signs all came from the Exmouth Junction concrete works when the halt was opened in September 1926, but the short platform had no shelter. As with Yarde Halt, passengers were advised to travel in the leading coach of Down trains and the rear coach of Up trains, and drivers were instructed 'to bring the trains to a stand at the halt platform accordingly'. *Robert Darlaston*

Ivatt '2MT' No. 41294 departs from Watergate into the woods with a single coach for Torrington. The 2-6-2T was at Exmouth Junction from June 1957 until March 1963.

Yarde Halt opened in July 1926 a year after the ND&CJLR itself. The cottages on the left were built and owned by the Devon Clay Company and about twenty of its employees travelled each day to Dunsbear Halt. It provided more passengers than any other station or halt on the line. The clay company paid for the train and hence no tickets were issued. The platform was only fifty feet long and therefore could only accommodate one coach; the shelter was built from standard Southern Railway prefabricated components.

No. 41216 at Dunsbear Halt with a freight from Torrington at a date between January 1963, when it came to Barnstaple Junction, and November 1964, when it moved to Exmouth Junction. No. 41216 was one of thirteen of the class transferred to the Western Region following the takeover of the Southern lines by that Region in January 1963. They replaced the '2MT's that had been working in North Devon in the 1950s and which were transferred away to Southern Region sheds during 1963.

Dunsbear Halt was opened as part of the original ND&CJLR. It had a platform of local stone and two waiting rooms, one in stone and one wooden which was added later to cope with the large number of clayworkers who used the halt after a mile-long walk from their works.

No. 41283 crosses a mixed train at Petrockstow. Here the station was about a mile from the village. The early morning workmen's train from Torrington carrying men to Dunsbear Halt worked through to Petrockstow where the two brake composite coaches were stabled for the day. One returned on a lunchtime train and one later in the afternoon. The coaches were sent every week to Exmouth Junction for cleaning to remove the clay which the workers had brought in.

On another day, this time without a headcode disc, No. 41283 emits plenty of steam as it pauses at Petrockstow. Like Hatherleigh and Hole, the station had the standard ND&CJLR crossing loop with two platforms and two sidings in the goods yard. The station building was constructed from local stone and had a small wooden awning and there was no goods shed, only a cattle loading dock.

Although built by the ND&CJLR, Petrockstow had some L&SWR station fittings. For example, the lamp post with its 'barley twist' post and copper top with blue etched glass name tablet was a standard L&SWR item. No. 41313 crosses another member of the class, probably in 1963.

There is lots of activity at Meeth Halt which opened with the line in 1925. It had a stone-built waiting room but, unlike the other two halts, passenger traffic was sparse because it had no service for the clayworkers. However, it did have a single siding, the buffer stop of which is just visible on the extreme left of the picture. Note the absence of a cover on the corridor connection.

No. 41283 at Hole, a station that theoretically served the villages of Black Torrington, which was referred to on the enamel station signs, and also Sheepwash and Highampton, all of which were several miles away. The hamlet of Hole itself was actually four miles from the station. Alongside the standard ND&CJLR two-siding goods yard was a huge grain-drying shed, but this did not provide any traffic for the line and the main goods traffic flows in later years were for a local farmer and cattle dealer.

No. 41283 was built at Crewe in November 1950 and had vacuum controlled regulator equipment. Originally allocated to Wakefield, it then spent the next ten years at a number of different sheds in the North West before moving to Brighton in June 1961. No. 41283 was transferred to Barnstaple Junction in June 1963 and left for Yeovil in September 1964. The Halwill to Torrington trains had, since the mid-1950s, consisted of a single BCK (Brake Composite Corridor) providing both First and Second class accomodation, originally either of Maunsell or Bulleid design, but by the 1960s almost exclusively the latter.

Ivatt 2-6-2T No. 41214 with a mixed train conveying china clay wagons together with the clay workers' coach from Petrockstow, takes on water at Hatherleigh. Built at Crewe in September 1948, it reached the Southern Region in late 1961, initially at Plymouth Friary and then at Barnstaple Junction in January 1963. It still has a Friary 83H shed plate which suggests the picture was probably taken in early 1963 soon after its transfer to Barnstaple. No. 41214 moved to Templecombe in August 1964 and was withdrawn from the Somerset & Dorset shed in July 1965. Hatherleigh had the standard ND&CJLR configuration of a passing loop controlled by reduced signalling, with only a Home and Starter in each direction operated from a seven-lever frame on the Up platform. Tyers No. 6 instruments housed in the booking hall controlled the single line working to Petrockstow and Hole. Hatherleigh had the only water supply on the line between Torrington and Halwill, with a water column at the end of each platform replenished by water from the nearby River Lew pumped up twice weekly into a large tank on the embankment above the station. The station served the largest population centre on the ND&CJLR but it was almost two miles away from the town. The stone-built station building had a wooden canopy utilising the roof trusses and housed the booking office, booking hall, lamp room, goods store and gents toilet.

Halwill Junction

Ex-L&SWR 'T9' 4-4-0 No. 30711 at Halwill Junction on 4th July 1957. It was built by Dübs & Co. in June 1899 and was allocated to Exmouth Junction from December 1951 until withdrawal in August 1959. The coaching set further down the platform will probably have been detached from the rear of No. 30711's train, one part going to Bude and the other to Padstow behind the 'T9'. The signal box on the left of the picture was built in 1879 and extended in 1925 to house the equipment for the ND&CJLR line to Torrington opened in that year. The typical North Devon stone goods shed has a canopy for protection from the elements and goods traffic looks healthy, although since this is a junction station yard much of this could be 'in-transit'.

When the North Devon and Cornwall Junction Light Railway line to Torrington was opened it came into Halwill Junction alongside the track from Bude and ran into its own branch platform where 2-6-2T No. 41283 has just arrived from Torrington. The guard is laden down with what was probably the entire contents from his van as the driver has a quick word with him.

'N' Class 2-6-0 No. 31406 at Halwill Junction with a Bude to Okehampton service on 27th April 1963. It was one of the fifteen engines built in the early 1930s, almost ten years after the majority of the class. They were recognisable by their 'U1' pattern chimneys and domes, and 4,000 gallon tenders with turned-in tops. No. 31406 was transferred from Weymouth to Exmouth Junction in February 1962 and was withdrawn from there in September 1964.

No. 41214 in the branch bay at Halwill Junction, probably in summer 1963, on the Torrington service formed by a single Bulleid brake composite with a BR guards van attached at the rear to work back to Torrington. It was transferred from the London Midland Region in late 1961, firstly to Plymouth Friary and then on to Barnstaple Junction in January 1963, where it stayed until August 1964.

No. 80059 departs from Halwill Junction on a Padstow train in the early 1960s. Displaced by the Kent Coast electrification, nine BR Standard 2-6-4Ts were transferred to Exmouth Junction in June 1962, working the Exmouth and Sidmouth services and on the Bude Branch. They also substituted for 'N' Class 2-6-0s on the Ilfracombe and Torrington trains. On the dispersal of most of Exmouth Junction's steam allocation in September 1964 No. 80059 went to the Somerset & Dorset shed at Templecombe. On the right is the 'Junction Hotel' which is still there today and is now trading as the 'Junction Inn'. The line from Meldon Junction to Halwill Junction and westwards to Wadebridge and Bude was closed on 3rd October 1966.

Ivatt '2MT' 2-6-2T No. 41291 was the second of the class built with enlarged cylinder bores, increasing the tractive effort from 17,400lbs to 18,510lbs, and a taller and thinner chimney than on the earlier engines. It had arrived in the South West in March 1963, moving from its only previous shed at Stewarts Lane to Exmouth Junction. Its stay in Devon was quite short and it went to the Somerset & Dorset at Templecombe in June 1965.

2 – Plymouth

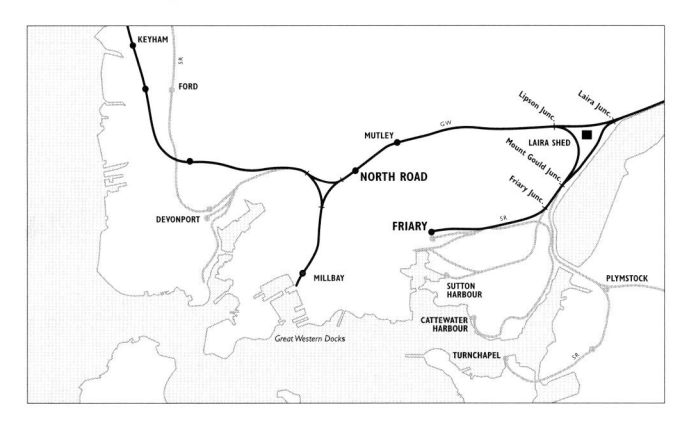

The first railway into Plymouth was the broad gauge South Devon Railway in 1847 which became the Great Western main line, the latter formally taking it over in 1876. In the same year the London & South Western Railway reached there, running from Exeter via Okehampton and then over the Great Western on mixed gauge rails from Lydford into what was a temporary terminus at Devonport, before a joint station at North Road was opened the following year. It was not until 1891 that the L&SWR opened a new terminus at Friary, accessed via running powers over the GWR between Devonport Junction and Lipson Junction, but using a new line built from Lydford to just west of North Road, opened in 1890. The result of this was that North Road, like Exeter St. Davids, was a station where the trains to London could depart in either direction, depending on whether they were bound for Waterloo or Paddington.

North Road

Viewed from the lane running alongside Plymouth North Road station, No. 5053 *Earl Cairns* from Newton Abbot Shed pilots a 'Hall' away from Platform 7, the 'Castle' just assisting over the South Devon banks as the train is probably well over the limit for an unassisted 'Hall'. No. 5053 was built in 1936 as *Bishop's Castle* but was renamed in August 1937. It had a Hawksworth tender from December 1952 until March 1954, and then again from December 1954 when it was transferred from Stafford Road to Newton Abbot.

Laira have turned out their own No. 6010 *King Charles I* in superb condition and it stands in Platform 8 at North Road with three strengthening coaches, awaiting the arrival into Platform 7 of the 9.30am from Falmouth. On arrival, the engine from Cornwall will come off and go to Laira Shed, allowing No. 6010 to add its coaches to the train before leaving for Paddington. The neat chalked '623' reporting number was sometimes used at Laira in place of the customary metal numbers in a metal frame. We were told that there was a specially made series of stencils for these chalked reporting numbers kept at Laira Shed.

Laira's No. 1010 *County of Caernarvon* has worked into Platform 7 at North Road from Penzance with the Paddington-bound 'Cornish Riviera'. The fireman is about to uncouple from the leading coach in order for No. 1010 to run light engine out to its home shed; he has already changed the lamp on the front buffer beam. The date is in or about 1954, No. 1010 having a double chimney from January 1957. There will be a 'King' waiting over on Platform 8 with the strengthening coaches ready to bring them over before taking this train onwards to Paddington. Much-favoured for these workings, the 'County' Class engines were well liked, often substituting for a 'Castle', but were later replaced on these duties by the newly-allocated members of the 'Britannia' Class.

Laira's No. 6010 *King Charles I* sets off from Plymouth for Paddington on 16th January 1954. No. 6010's driver is looking back to check that all is well. There is no pilot engine attached, the load being within the ten coach maximum for an unassisted 'King' over the banks to Newton Abbot. The large red brick building in the background is the Royal Eye Infirmary which was operational in this capacity until 2013. A couple of engines wait in the siding for their next call to duty, with the site of the long abandoned Mutley station to the right of the leading coach.

No. 6023 *King Edward II* setting off from Plymouth North Road in the early 'fifties at 12.30pm with the Paddington bound 'Cornish Riviera'. One of the biggest restoration jobs on an ex-Barry engine, No. 6023 was brought out of the scrapyard with its rear driving wheels cut-through after a derailment, and had been thought beyond repair. This was not the case, and after a twenty-year restoration it moved under its own power for the first time in 2011 and has since worked on the main line in single chimney form wearing BR blue livery.

Laira's No. 1010 *County of Caernarvon* waits in Platform 8 at Plymouth North Road at the head of the strengthening coaches for the 9.30am from Falmouth, which it will add here once the train arrives from Cornwall on the adjacent Platform 7. The neatly chalked '623' reporting number would have been applied at Laira. The driver is heading down the platform with a tea urn in his hand, doubtless making his way to the station buffet for a refill. There is clearly plenty of time left because the Express Passenger lamp headcode has not yet been added by No. 1010's fireman, and a number of doors on the carriages are still open.

The heavily loaded 12 noon 'North Mail' from Penzance, the 3.45pm from Plymouth, sets off from Plymouth North Road past the Royal Eye Infirmary on 5th August 1956. The train conveyed a Glasgow portion which reached its destination at 7.30am the following morning, having waited at Crewe from 11.25 pm until 1.04 am! Penzance allocated No. 6808 *Beenham Grange* is assisting Old Oak's No. 70018 *Flying Dutchman* to Newton Abbot over the South Devon banks. No. 70018 will work through to Bristol Temple Meads, where after a short stop over at Bath Road Shed, it and its crew will be rostered on a later passenger working from Temple Meads back home to Paddington. With the introduction of the 'Britannias', this duty was a regular for the Laira and Old Oak members of the class, taking over from the 'Kings' which had earlier been the mainstay of this working. The Royal Mail coach leading the formation will also come off at Bristol, returning to Plymouth the following morning. The notice just visible on the railings in front of the waiting '43xx' 2-6-0 requested drivers of engines waiting in the siding to remember the patients in the Royal Eye Hospital on the other side of the road, and to keep smoke and noise to a minimum.

On another Saturday during the Summer Workings, probably also in 1956, Laira's No. 6008 *King James II* pilots a 'Britannia' through Mutley Cutting into Plymouth North Road with the 10.35am relief from Paddington to the down 'Cornish Riviera Limited'. No. 6008 had worked the 10.30am departure, the 'Riviera' itself, to Newton Abbot and has come on to this relief there to work back to Plymouth because the 'Riviera' did not stop there on Summer Saturdays. Unlike the picture on the following page, No. 6008's fireman has correctly removed the '130' reporting number from its frame, together with the 'Cornish Riviera Limited' headboard.

A Summer Saturday spectacular at Plymouth on 5th August 1956 with Laira's No. 6025 *King Henry III* pilot to Old Oak Common's No. 6019 *King Henry V* approaching North Road station with the 10.35am departure from Paddington. As shown by the headboard and reporting number, No. 6025 had worked from Paddington to Newton Abbot with the 10.30am 'Cornish Riviera Limited' but because this train did not stop at Plymouth on Summer Saturdays, running non-stop to Truro, it had come off at Newton Abbot. There it awaited arrival of the second portion of the train which had left London just five minutes behind the first, and was coupled ahead of the train engine, leading to the rare sight of two 'Kings' double-heading.

The Royal Eye Infirmary is in the background as the two 'Kings' run past the photographer towards North Road station. It was no wonder with all those engines in the siding that a notice on those railings asked enginemen to keep smoke and noise to a minimum for the benefit of patients!

Running into Plymouth North Road on 30th July 1956 with a freight, No. 34004 *Yeovil* will probably have come from the Southern line at Friary, joining the Western Region main line at Lipson Junction, and now running the 'Wrong Way' to Exeter on the Southern route via Okehampton. No. 34004 was allocated to Exmouth Junction from new in 1945 and would be one of several 'Light Pacifics' transferred to the South Eastern section when called into Eastleigh for rebuilding, moving to Bricklayers Arms when it emerged without streamlining in February 1958. It still has the rail near the top of the smoke deflectors which was used to hold the 'Devon Belle' name boards. Pannier tank No. 8709 on the left also moved away, transferring from Laira to Chester at the end of 1958.

An unusual shot of 'T9' 4-4-0 No. 30717 double-heading 'U' Class No. 31804 on a 'City of Plymouth Holiday Express' waiting to leave Platform 6 at North Road on 3rd September 1956, bound for Ilfracombe via the Southern Region North Dartmoor line. These Specials were arranged at that time in order to provide attractive days out for the citizens of Plymouth at seaside locations in Cornwall and Devon, with specially discounted fares. Mr Anthony, the Stationmaster, complete with bowler hat, is chatting to the crew of the 'T9', and the sun is already shining, but then it always did in those days! No. 30717 was built for the L&SWR by Dübs & Co. in September 1899. It moved to the West Country in 1937 and was allocated mainly to Exmouth Junction, with short spells at Wadebridge and Barnstaple in the early 1950s. It was withdrawn in July 1961.

Churchward 'Mogul' No. 6385, built by Robert Stephenson & Hawthorn Ltd of Newcastle in August 1921, heading a rake of Southern Region coaches including a CCT van. It was allocated to Exeter from June 1954 until November 1959 when it was transferred to Reading.

An unusual pairing of motive power on Saturday 15th September 1956 due almost certainly to a shortage of locomotives available at Laira Shed. No. 70016 *Ariel* is coupled ahead of a '5101' 2-6-2T on a heavily loaded express, as they set off from North Road. This is probably a relief to the 3.45pm to the North of England because it has a full brake leading the train. The load is clearly well over the maximum for an unassisted 'Britannia' over the South Devon banks to Newton Abbot and, conforming with regulations, the 'pilot' engine, being a 2-6-2T, has been correctly coupled inside the train engine rather than ahead of it. No. 70016 was allocated to Laira from August 1953 until the end of 1956 when it was transferred to Cardiff Canton.

'Hall' No. 5977 *Beckford Hall* will assist 'Warship' No. D601 *Ark Royal* over the South Devon banks on the Up 'Cornish Riviera' in August 1958. The heavyweight diesel-hydraulic had been delivered from the North British Locomotive Company in March 1958 and was allocated to Laira in June of that year. No. D601 will probably work through to Paddington, returning with the 6.30pm Paddington-Bristol and then the 2.55pm ex-Manchester from Bristol to Plymouth.

This is the eastern end of North Road's Platform 7 with a rather uncared for 'Modified Hall' No. 6990 *Witherslack Hall* acting as pilot to North British 'Warship' No. D604 *Cossack*, probably on a Paddington-bound working. Steam piloting of diesels over the South Devon banks was frowned upon by those in authority as it was considered that the ingress of smoke and steam into the diesels' air intakes would cause damage to the power units, but the rule was often broken, as we see here! No. 6990 was rescued from Barry scrapyard in 1975 and restored to steam in 1986 at the Great Central Railway where it has been based ever since. It took part in the 1948 Interchange Trials in the mixed traffic category, working from Marylebone to Sheffield.

A long-standing Friary engine since 1937, 'M7' 0-4-4T No. 30035, in August 1958, just a month before the ex-Southern Railway station closed to passengers. It is working from that station through North Road heading for the Southern Region line to North Cornwall, probably to Tavistock. No. 30035 was built at Nine Elms in May 1898 and was an 'M7/1', with short frames and sandboxes on the front splashers. It was transferred to Eastleigh in January 1960 and then a year later to Feltham, where it was mainly employed on empty stock workings out of Waterloo.

Pannier tank No. 3686, emerging from Mutley tunnel with a local trip freight, was transferred to Laira from Taunton in February 1945 and stayed until April 1960 went it moved to Chester. On the left is the site of the former Mutley station which was in use from 1871, before North Road was opened, and did not close until July 1939. On the right, the walkway to the Down platform is still visible.

The fifth of the heavyweight A1A-A1A North British built 'Warships' No. D604 *Cossack* in the early 1960s. This picture was taken before it was modified with vertical air intakes on the two upper pairs of three air intakes in January 1961.

The family resemblance of the smaller Type '2' to the 'D600s' is clear, but the chopped-off cab front detracted from their appearance compared with the nose end on the 'Warships'. No. D6314 arrives with a stopping service from Exeter with a train composed of three green Southern Region Mark 1 coaches with an ex-LM&SR Stanier Brake Third bringing up the rear.

CHAPTER 2 - PLYMOUTH

The North British Type '2s' often operated in pairs in Cornwall during their early years where their maximum permitted speed of 75mph was not an operational issue. No's D6322 and D6321 entered service in April 1960 and their condition suggests this picture was probably taken later in that year.

Steam and diesel combinations working over the South Devon banks were common for only two or three years in the early 1960s. 'Warship' No. D817 *Foxhound* will be assisted by a 'Grange' 4-6-0 on this Up working. The diesel entered traffic in March 1960 and was allocated to Laira depot until March 1967. This picture was taken before it received overhead warning flashes in December 1961. *Foxhound* had a working life of just over a decade and was withdrawn in October 1971 having covered 1,078,000 miles.

One of the five heavyweight North British built 'Warships', No. D603 *Conquest* at Plymouth on 4th July 1961. Apart from the early acceptance trials and testing in 1958 of No's D600 and D601 working from Swindon, all five were allocated to Laira, where their idiosyncrasies were well-known by maintenance staff. The operating statistics included in the minutes of the BR Motive Power Committee showed that for long periods in 1959-62, two and sometimes three of the five locomotives were out of service. After 1962, they were stopped from working east of Newton Abbot and therefore spent all their time in the far South West, except for a few weeks in late-1967 when three of them had a brief sojourn in South Wales prior to their withdrawal at the end of that year. Although their already limited use on top duty passenger work continued to decline as the 'Westerns' took over most of the West of England work from 1964, the 'D600s' still worked the prestige duties occasionally, right up to their demise. The lash-up support for the train reporting number frame on No. D603 did nothing for the front-end appearance and the brackets to support the train headboard are just dangling. Yellow warning panels were applied when it went into works in February 1962 and 4-character train identification indicators were fitted in October 1965.

CHAPTER 2 - PLYMOUTH

'West Country' No. 34011 *Tavistock* is watched by a group of children as it runs towards the 183 yard long Mutley tunnel in July 1961. Since the Southern's Friary station had closed to passenger traffic three years earlier and there is a 'Plymouth' label in the window of the first coach, this is probably an ECS working to Laira carriage sidings.

'4575' 2-6-2T No. 5541 at Plymouth with a Launceston train in 1961. This engine was a regular on the branch during its last two years in service up to withdrawal in July 1962. In 1961 Laira had nine of these '4575' 2-6-2Ts to work the passenger and freight trains of which five, including No. 5541, were auto-fitted and took over the Autotrains up to Tavistock South in place of the '64xx' Panniers and '14xx' 0-4-2Ts. No. 5541 is now preserved on the Dean Forest Railway.

'4575' No. 5511 setting off from North Road for Tavistock and Launceston on 1st September 1961. It was transferred to Laira in October 1958 from Bristol Bath Road and was withdrawn at the end of 1961. It appears to be carrying oil cans and stores on the front framing ahead of the steam pipe. The building under construction is the new 'Rail House', built when it was proposed that Plymouth was to be a Railway Administrative Centre, but later left virtually empty for many years when the centre was changed to Swindon. It is still almost empty today!

Three views, one opposite, taken on the same day, show the diversity of motive power on view at North Road in 1961.

North British Type '2' diesel hydraulic No. D6331 was built in July 1960 and worked for just over ten years, being withdrawn in March 1971. It was one of the last of the class built without route indicators.

Rebuilt 'Battle of Britain' No. 34056 *Croydon* runs in with what the photographer recorded as a local from Exeter. However, it is displaying BR(S) discs positioned to Western Region configuration, signifying an empty coaching stock (ECS) train, probably from Friary. The headcode will be changed to the Southern Region Plymouth-Waterloo code at North Road station. No. 34056 was one of the last batch of engines rebuilt, emerging from Eastleigh on Christmas Eve 1960.

'43xx' 2-6-0 No. 7335 with a train of empty china clay wagons returning to Cornwall. The wooden 5-plank wagons carry tarpaulins over their empty interiors, presumably to protect the wagons from contamination – a steam engine was a dirty machine! The Mogul was built in 1932 as No. 9313 and became No. 7335 in August 1958 when the concrete weights behind the front buffer beam were removed. It was allocated to Laira between June 1958 and November 1961.

'N' Class 2-6-0 No. 31838 waits with the relief for the 2.25pm to Waterloo on 28th August 1962. It was one of the large group of the class shedded at Exmouth Junction that were built at Ashford from kits of parts purchased from the Government. These originated when the Association of Railway Locomotive Engineers attempted to produce standard locomotive types for use by all British railway companies and the Government selected the design to be produced by the former munitions factory at Woolwich Arsenal as an alternative to closing the factory after the end of the First World War. The Government found few takers for them and the Southern Railway was able to buy fifty sets of parts very cheaply, and hence these engines became known as 'Woolworths'; No. 31838 worked from Exmouth Junction right up to withdrawal in February 1964.

A good view of the extent of North Road station with its three double slips on the Down side and carriage sidings on the Up side. Note also the newly erected tall floodlight. 'Warship' No. D822 *Hercules* departs northwards with the Up 'Cornishman' in August 1961. The green livery of the 'Warships' was relieved only by the grey lining band on the side and the front end looks very uninspiring. In the background, the 154 feet high 'Rail House' is under construction and there is a '45xx' and another 'Warship' awaiting departure eastwards.

CHAPTER 2 - PLYMOUTH

At the other end of the station, approaching from Cornwall, No. D808 *Centaur* was one of the early 'Warships' built with a steam-style three position reporting panel. Its original plain green livery has been modified by the addition of a yellow warning panel in March 1962, but it did not receive a four-character train identification panel until the end of 1964. The main line to Cornwall over the Royal Albert Bridge curved sharply and is visible in the background to the right of the diesel; the lines on the left are to Millbay, the parcels and freight distribution centre, and also served the former GWR Docks from where the Ocean Mail Special Transatlantic boat trains would begin their non-stop run up to Paddington.

Old Oak Common's No. 7018 *Drysllwyn Castle* has been well coaled at Laira for its journey back towards London accompanied by 'Warship' No. D829 *Magpie* on 21st May 1963.

In its original maroon livery, No. D1010 *Western Campaigner* in June 1964 with an express for Paddington. It was the last 'Western' built with no yellow warning panels; these had been added in March 1963.

'Hymek' Type '3's were the least common of the Western Region mainline hydraulic classes in the far South West and were very rare in Cornwall. No. D7100 has brought in a westbound express from the London Midland Region in August 1964. This was the last of the 101 locomotives built at Gorton by Beyer, Peacock and entered service in February 1964, allocated initially to Newton Abbot, but transferred to Laira three months later, for the next two years.

CHAPTER 2 - PLYMOUTH

Brush Type '4' No. D1754 had been released to traffic from the Brush Works at Loughborough on August 19th 1964 and allocated to Landore. It still looks brand new as it waits to depart with an express to Paddington early the following month. No. D1754 became No. 47160, No. 47605 and finally No. 47746 under the TOPS renumbering.

A three-car Birmingham Railway Carriage & Wagon Co. DMU, later Class '118', working a Plymouth-Penzance service in September 1964. Nearest the camera is Motor Brake Second No. W51306 with Trailer Composite No. W59473 in the centre, but the third car has been replaced by a Gloucester Railway Carriage & Wagon Co. single unit No. W55011, no doubt due to a medium term failure. There were always more single car units than needed, so even from this early date they were used to deputise for failures.

No. D1015 *Western Champion* at Plymouth in March 1965 was still in the golden ochre livery which lasted until later that year. The livery was proposed by the late Brian Haresnape as an alternative to the standard British Railways diesel green but was not taken up, with *Western Champion* remaining the sole example. In 1979, No. D1015 was rescued, literally at the final hour before it was due to be cut-up at Swindon, by the Diesel Traction Group. It was in appalling condition and after many years' effort and following what amounted to virtually a complete rebuild, *Western Champion* was restored to main line condition by 2002 and has worked extensively on railtours since then.

'Warship' No. D864 *Zambesi* after arrival with the 8.30am Paddington-Penzance. It was built in Glasgow by the North British Locomotive Company and entered traffic in May 1962 allocated to Laira depot. In the background is the 154 feet high 'Rail House', built between 1956 and 1962 at the same time as North Road station was being rebuilt. It has ten storeys and is one of the three tallest buildings in Plymouth.

'Warship' No. D827 *Kelly* in August 1968 with the 08.40 Penzance to Wolverhampton express. Note that the overhead live wire flashes are missing from the side of the locomotive; when these were replaced they appeared in front of the doors rather than behind which made it unique among Swindon-built 'Warships'. The Multiple Working equipment which had been taken off has reappeared because of the paired diagrams for the accelerated West of England services introduced in 1968.

Waiting to depart eastwards, No. D1037 *Western Empress* in blue livery with small yellow warning panels which it carried from January 1967 until June 1971. Only seven 'Westerns' were painted in this interim style of blue before the standard version with full yellow ends and cab window surrounds was applied to the class. The top of the Royal Eye Infirmary is just visible behind North Road East signal box.

Class '45' No. 30 runs towards Mutley Tunnel in a snowy January 1969.

Class '46' No. D163 *Leicestershire and Derbyshire Yeomanry* with a south-west to north-east express in September 1969. It is in the so-called 'economy' plain green without a lower bodyline stripe after a re-paint carried out at either Toton or the Brush works at Loughborough. It was one of the last to retain green livery.

CHAPTER 2 - PLYMOUTH

North British Type '2' No. D6307 in September 1969 illustrates the prominent headcode boxes fitted to the earlier members of the class in the mid-1960s. These were slightly different, being more bulky and positioned higher up the cab front than the later design. After the first few locomotives had been fitted with these boxes it was realised they were a rain trap and the mechanism inside rusted up, which made it almost impossible for crews to set the numerals and letters in the desired positions. A revised and more expensive solution with the boxes sunk into the nose had to be introduced but some locomotives, including No. D6307, remained unmodified. Note there is a blue TOPS data panel on the shabby green livery.

A Sunday diversion at Lipson Junction on 11th March 1956 for Laira's 'Britannia' No. 70019 Lightning with the 10.10am from Plymouth to Paddington. Lipson Junction Signal Box is on the left and the signalman there has taken No. 70019 off the Up main line onto the Up Goods due to engineering work further down towards Laira Junction. Four 'Britannias' were allocated to Laira at this time, the others being No's 70016/21/24, but all were transferred away to Cardiff Canton at the end of 1956.

Laira's No. 5098 *Clifford Castle* runs along the estuary of the River Plym on 4th March 1956 with the Sunday 'North to West' express which it had taken over at Bristol Temple Meads. The last two coaches, with roofboards, are probably through coaches from Glasgow, added to this train at Crewe. The distant signal has not cleared and No. 5098's driver has shut off steam in case he has not got the road through Laira Junction, which is just ahead. *Clifford Castle* was the first of the post-war 'Castles', built in May 1946, and spent most of its career at Laira, finally leaving in January 1962.

CHAPTER 2 - PLYMOUTH

No. 6010 *King Charles I* has also been checked by the same distant signal as No. 5098 in the photograph on the previous page. The date is Wednesday 25th April 1956 and No. 6010 is working home on the 1.30pm from Paddington, due into Plymouth at 6.25pm. The line just visible on the extreme left was part of the 4ft 6in. gauge Lee Moor tramway, running down from Lee Moor to Cattewater and worked in days past by horses hauling china clay from the Lee Moor china clay workings. It crossed the main line at Laira Junction and by historical precedent had priority over the Great Western main line; commercial operations on the tramway ceased in 1945 but the owning company did not wish to relinquish the right of way and token movements continued until 26th August 1960, the last time the Lee Moor Tramway horses pulled wagons across the main line.

A group of spotters watch No. 5906 *Lawton Hall* running up to Lipson Junction passing the Laira coaling stage with a Down express in the early 1960s. This picture was taken from the top of the steps leading down to the pedestrian underpass below the main line, with the site of the long closed Laira Halt visible on the left. The main line was virtually at sea level approaching Laira Junction and quite flat past the shed and Laira Halt but, thereafter, there was a steady climb for 1½ miles at 1 in 77, then 1 in 83 up to Mutley Tunnel before the descent into North Road station. No. 5906 had been allocated to Reading Shed since 1954 and was withdrawn from there in May 1962.

Laira

No. 1365 was one of three of the class of 0-6-0STs allocated to Laira for use at Millbay Docks, the former Great Western Railway commercial dock, and at the former Millbay station, the centre for freight distribution in the Plymouth area. Laira's steam crane on the left was used for clearing ash from the coaling line in addition to other tasks. No. 1365, pictured in Laira Shed yard on September 16th 1951, was transferred to Swindon in April 1955, where it was used within the Works complex.

Laira's No. 1010 *County of Caernarvon* in February 1956 is suspended under the hoist with its bogie removed and has been separated from its tender. No. 1010 moved to Laira from Old Oak Common at the end of 1950 and stayed at the Plymouth shed until October 1959.

Sunday 18th March 1956 with Old Oak Common's No. 4704 on Laira Shed in this morning shot. Churchward's '47xx' 2-8-0s were nicknamed the 'Night Owls' because of their regular use on overnight freight workings to and from the Capital. No. 4704 bears the signs of having recently been through the Works, despite the damaged smokebox door number plate. It is too early in the year for Summer Specials and it may have worked down overnight, but it has a single 'ordinary stopping train' lamp in position so may be on an ex-Works 'Running-In' duty, possibly from Bristol.

It is the evening of 24th April 1956 and on the coaling line No. 6026 *King John* has had its fire dropped, as shown by the ash spillage on the cabside. The gentleman in a splendid hat is one of Laira's firedroppers, complete with his long-handled shovel. No. 6026 will have worked down from Paddington and now that its fire has been cleared it will be moved up in order to have its tender re-coaled and probably its smokebox cleared of accumulated ash.

A very dirty and work-stained 'Star' No. 4062 *Malmesbury Abbey*, then allocated to Swindon Shed, has been re-coaled at Laira Shed on 9th May 1956. It was near the end of its working life and was one of only three 'Stars' still in service at this period of time, and was taken out of traffic six months later after the end of the summer timetable. It is most unusually coupled to a Hawksworth flat-sided tender.

Three 'Kings' at Laira when the photographer Peter Kerslake's notes show that there were no less than ten on shed that day! No. 6004 *King George III*, nearest the camera, is probably booked for the 4.10pm to Paddington, and from the faint '605' on the smokebox door looks as though it has recently worked the 8.30am to London. The middle engine is Old Oak's No. 6012 *King Edward VI* which with '665' chalked on its smokebox door, is for the 3.45pm 'North Mail' (the 12 noon from Penzance) which it will take to Bristol Temple Meads to work from there back home to Paddington on an express later that same evening. Furthest from the camera is Laira's No. 6023 *King Edward II* with its 'Cornish Riviera' headboard already in place, and this will be the first of this trio to come off shed for its non-stop run up to Paddington.

It is Whit Saturday 19th May 1956 and Old Oak Common's No. 6012 *King Edward VI* has worked down to Plymouth on the 11.0am relief from Paddington, running behind the 'Cornish Riviera' by 30 minutes or so. On Laira's coaling line No. 6012 is having its smokebox and tubes cleared, is being re-coaled and has already had its fire 'dropped' as evidenced by the ash on the cabside.

A trio of 'Castles' on shed at Laira on Whitsun Sunday 20th May 1956, with a fourth one in the background too! Devonport's Navy Days were held early that year, over this weekend, rather than in the usual August, and Cardiff Canton's No. 5054 *Earl of Ducie* in the foreground had come down on a Navy Day special from Wales. Penzance-allocated No. 4099 *Kilgerran Castle* had come up from Cornwall on a similar working. Bristol Bath Road's No. 5063, *Earl Baldwin* is on the centre road. A fitter is attending to No. 5054.

Laira's coaling line on 1st April 1956 has an unusual visitor in the unfamiliar shape of '8F' No. 48410 from Bristol St.Philips Marsh, where it had been allocated since the previous August. The Stanier 2-8-0 was one of the eighty built by the Great Western Railway at Swindon during the war.

When all the 'Kings' were taken out of service in early 1956 after cracks were discovered in some of the bogie frames, four Stanier Pacifics were hastily sent to Old Oak Common from the London Midland Region to assist on the Paddington to Plymouth and Wolverhampton services. No. 46210 *Lady Patricia* worked the down 'Cornish Riviera' from Paddington to Plymouth on 10th February 1956, but suffered a collapsed firebox brick arch on the way down and was awaiting replacement bricks in Laira's Long Shed with No. 6017 *King Edward IV*, minus its bogie, alongside. Laira's fitters have taken the opportunity to replace No. 6017's piston valve rings whilst awaiting the return of its bogie from Swindon Works where strengthening work on it would have been carried out.

This is an evening shot from 1st May 1956 as St. Blazey-allocated '5101' Class 2-6-2T No. 5193 waits for permission to come off Laira Shed to work back down to Cornwall on a freight. The little corrugated iron hut housed the telephone which the fireman of an engine coming off shed would use to get permission from the signalman at Lipson Junction to come up on to the Southern lines to and from Friary, which are in the foreground. From there, the engines would run up to Lipson Junction, out of the picture on the left. The River Plym is in the background, with the Southern flanks of Dartmoor visible on the horizon with Saltram Park on the far side of the Plym in the right background.

Old Oak Common's 'Britannia' No. 70017 *Arrow* coming off Laira Shed on 5th May 1956 by what was commonly known as the 'Speedway' on its way up to North Road to work the 7.50pm fitted freight and 'Perishables' through to Bristol, from where it would later work home to Paddington. No. 70017's fireman is waiting in the little hut between the signals waiting for permission to come off shed and up on to the Southern line to Friary before crossing over and running tender first up to North Road. Laira's Running Shed, with its oil refuelling tanks are on the left and as usual for a Saturday there is plenty of motive power on shed.

The first twelve Swindon-built 'Warships' originally had steam-style frames to carry the three-digit train reporting numbers then in use on the Western Region. Those on No. D805 *Benbow* were replaced by 4-character train identification indicators in March 1964. No. D805 had worked the accelerated 'Bristolian' on 15th June 1959, the first day of the new timetable. With an 8-coach load, it reached Bristol in a net time of 91 minutes; this was nine minutes better than the accelerated schedule and was almost certainly the fastest run yet made from Paddington to Bristol, with a maximum speed of 95mph. *Benbow* was outside Laira New (or Long) Shed on 2nd July 1960; this four-road shed had been built in 1931 under one of the Government financial incentives. Two roads were adapted for use by diesel traction in July 1958 and the other pair in December 1959.

No. D1004 *Western Crusader* at Laira on 20th June 1962 was only a month old when this picture was taken. Three Swindon-built and four Crewe-built 'Westerns' originally had this green livery and No. D1004 was one of only three in the class never to carry maroon livery, going straight into blue in February 1967.

CHAPTER 2 - PLYMOUTH

A picture taken from Astor Park at Mount Gould on 21st September 1966 shows the Laira Diesel depot which was opened on 13th March 1962. The depot comprised three adjoining buildings: a four-road servicing and maintenance shed, a two-road heavy maintenance shed where engines could be removed, and a three-road servicing shed where locomotives could be inspected and refuelled. The River Plym, with Saltram Park on its far bank forms an attractive background and the tree-lined Embankment Road leading into Plymouth lies between the shed and the Plym. The southern fringes of Lee Moor and Dartmoor are just visible in the far distance. The houses on the skyline at Efford were part of the very first post-war housing development in the City of Plymouth, and had one of the best views of any Council houses in the country!

Swindon-built 'Warship' No. D816 *Eclipse* alongside a North British-built 'D833' in the new diesel maintenance shop on 22nd March 1962. Laira was one of four 'Heavy' maintenance depots with facilities to lift diesel-hydraulic engines and transmissions, and train-heating boilers and it could also undertake bogie changes and tyre-turning. The depot carried out general scheduled maintenance on a large proportion of the Western Region hydraulic fleet, which involved the periodical inspection, changing, dismantling and cleaning of specified components.

Crewe-built No. D1040 *Western Queen* at Laira in July 1968. It was the first 'Western' to be involved in a major collision when it hit a freight train at Knowle & Dorridge in August 1963 while deputising for one of the diesel Pullman trains on the 'Birmingham Pullman'. The cab which was damaged had no headboard clips above the indicator panel. No. D1040 retained its maroon livery until April 1970.

A view from the concrete footbridge which spanned the Laira Junction to Friary running lines at the South West corner of the shed of No. D6323 at Laira in 1969. The staining on the central bodyside was caused by the use of 'Dromas', an anti-corrosion inhibitor which was added to the boiler water feed and engine cooling water, and which escaped in the steam that emerged when the steam generator safety valve lifted, leaving the condensed water to run down the side of the locomotive. It was extremely effective at removing paint, and also the skin of shed staff who came into contact with it.

Class '22' No. D6318 at Laira on 10th May 1970 in Rail Blue with full yellow ends. Like No. D6323 above, its paintwork has also suffered from the use of the 'Dromas' anti-corrosion chemical. No. D6318 was withdrawn in May 1971.

The Western Region 'Hymek' and North British Type '2' hydraulics which were prevalent during the 1960s in the South West were ousted by surplus Sulzer Type '2's transferred from the London Midland Region. The last Class '25', No. 7677, built in May 1967 at Derby, is pictured at Laira in 1973. It was part of an order given to Beyer, Peacock, but their precarious financial position led to the company asking to be released from the final eighteen locomotives. No. 7677 moved to the Western Region in July 1971, initially to Newport and then to Laira in October. It spent part of 1972 at Bristol and Cardiff but returned to Laira by the end of the year; it became No. 25327 under TOPS, returned to the London Midland Region in August 1975 and was withdrawn in February 1984.

Friary

The London & South Western Railway opened its Plymouth terminus at Friary in 1891 and all trains except those on the Turnchapel Branch went via the Great Western North Road station, through which the L&SWR had running powers. It had four platforms, two of which were shorter bays, and as well as through services to Waterloo, it handled trains to Turnchapel and to Tavistock together with a Railmotor service in the local area. Friary station closed to passenger services in September 1958 and trains then used the former GWR station at North Road.

This picture was taken from the road bridge at the eastern side of Friary station in the early 'fifties, with 'M7' 0-4-4T No. 30035 as station pilot making up stock for an outgoing working. Southern Region trains leaving here would run on the triangle past the Western Region shed at Laira before joining that Region's main line from Paddington at Lipson Junction and then running 'the wrong way' through North Road station, before taking the Southern line via Okehampton to Exeter and beyond. No. 30035 was built at Nine Elms in 1898 and had been at Friary Shed since 1937; it stayed there until early 1960 when it was transferred to Eastleigh. It was an 'M7/1', one of the short-framed engines with front sandboxes on the splashers.

All hands to the turntable at Friary Shed to turn 'T9' 4-4-0 No. 30715 and its 8-wheel 'watercart' tender in around 1954. It is in British Railways mixed traffic livery, black with red/white/grey lining, and has a SPL (Special) white route indicator disc. No. 30715 spent all of its working life in the South West and was allocated to Exmouth Junction Shed from June 1950 until withdrawn in July 1961. Friary Shed was rebuilt in 1908 with a new fifty foot turntable; engines larger than this 'T9' had to turn on the nearby triangle.

With its birds nest spark arrester 'Drummond'-designed ex-L&SWR 0-4-0T No.30083 was a product of Nine Elms works in 1908. The small-boilered 'B4', one of only three in service at the time, was at Friary Shed for only two years, from October 1951 until October 1953 when it was replaced by No. 30088, one of the earlier larger-boilered 'B4's.

No. 30088 on the approach to Lucas Terrace Halt, which was just by Friary Shed, on a trip working from the Turnchapel Branch and Cattedown wharves with a freight. The line from Lipson Junction to Friary station, which passed underneath, is just visible beyond the embankment, with Laira Shed out of sight on the left and Tothill Park in the left foreground. The diminutive tank worked from Friary until August 1958 alongside classmates No's 30089 and 30102, when they all joined No. 30083 at Eastleigh; another 'B4' No. 30094 was also at the Friary Shed at this time but was withdrawn in March 1957.

Ex-L&SWR Adams 'G6' 0-6-0T No. 30162 at Friary, its home shed until withdrawn in March 1958. The 1908 shed was a large three-road L&SWR 'glass house' building with a mechanical coaling plant and hoist.

L&SWR Adams 1891 design 'B4' 0-4-0T No. 30088 inside Friary Shed on 10th May 1958, with Drewry No. 11228 which went new to Friary in September 1957, and with four classmates took over the Devonport yard duties, which included freight trips to Keyham Dockyard via St.Budeaux. The diesel shunter stayed in Plymouth until February 1962, moving to Hither Green and then Ashford; it was renumbered in June 1963 as No. D2258. It was in service for less than thirteen years, a contrast with No. 30088 which had clocked-up almost 70 years when it was withdrawn in July 1959. Friary Shed itself closed in May 1963.

Keyham

Pictured in June 1959 at Keyham, adjacent to the Royal Naval Barracks and Dockyard, Laira's 0-6-0ST No. 1361 is on shunting duties, one of the tasks that the three diminutive saddle tanks at Laira were often rostered to perform. It was at Laira until February 1960 when it was transferred to Weymouth.

Another photograph of No. 1361 on the same day hard at work at what was then the very busy Keyham, which was situated between Plymouth and the Tamar Bridge. What looks like a Naval Ambulance is on the extreme left, and the Ford is parked where many sailors would leave their cars covered for protection whilst they were away at sea, in an unofficial parking area. It was here that one of the 'Hall' Class, No. 4911 *Bowden Hall*, was destroyed by a bomb during the Second World War.

Millbay Docks

These two pictures and the one on the following page show one of Laira's 0-6-0STs, No. 1363, coupled to a GWR shunter's truck at Plymouth Millbay Docks. The six engines of the class were built in 1910 to operate sidings and dock lines where the sharp curvature necessitated a very short wheelbase engine. They were an updated version of the '1392' class which had originated on the Cornwall Minerals Railway, and were the last saddle tanks to be built at Swindon.

Laira Shed had three of these little saddletanks in the mid 'fifties, and one would work at Millbay, where there was a small single road engine shed, although they were also employed on other freight duties in and around Plymouth as seen on the previous pages. Millbay docks, just down from Millbay station, was where the Trans-Atlantic liners, running between New York and France and calling into Plymouth Sound en-route, would have mail offloaded by tenders running out to the ships from here. The saddle tanks marshalled the coaches for the Ocean Mail Trains, but their daily bread-and-butter work was spent on the large amount of perishable, grain and ordinary goods traffic. No. 1363 was withdrawn in November 1962 and was purchased for preservation by the Great Western Society; it is currently at Didcot awaiting overhaul.

3 – Southern Region – Cornwall

Most of the Southern Region lines in Cornwall were built by the North Cornwall Railway, with the exception of the Callington Branch, the Bodmin & Wadebridge Railway and the line from Halwill Junction to Bude which was built by the Devon & Cornwall Railway. Unusually, the North Cornwall maintained its nominal independence until the 1923 grouping, although it was operated from the outset by the London & South Western Railway. Authorised in the 1880s, it was not completed until nearly twenty years later. The Bodmin & Wadebridge had been operating since 1834 but it was not joined to the rest of the British railway system until 1895 when the North Cornwall reached there.

Callington

The nine mile-long branch from Bere Alston to Callington opened in 1908 following the extension and conversion to standard gauge of the 3ft 6in. gauge East Cornwall Minerals Railway between Callington and Calstock, which was two miles from Bere Alston. The junction at Bere Alston faced Okehampton, whereas most of the traffic was for Plymouth, which was in the other direction, thereby mitigating through trains. In the 1950s, there were two through coaches from the branch to Plymouth Friary which were attached to services on the main line at Bere Alston. The line survives today as far as Gunnislake which is now the terminus for the 'Tamar Valley Line' from Plymouth.

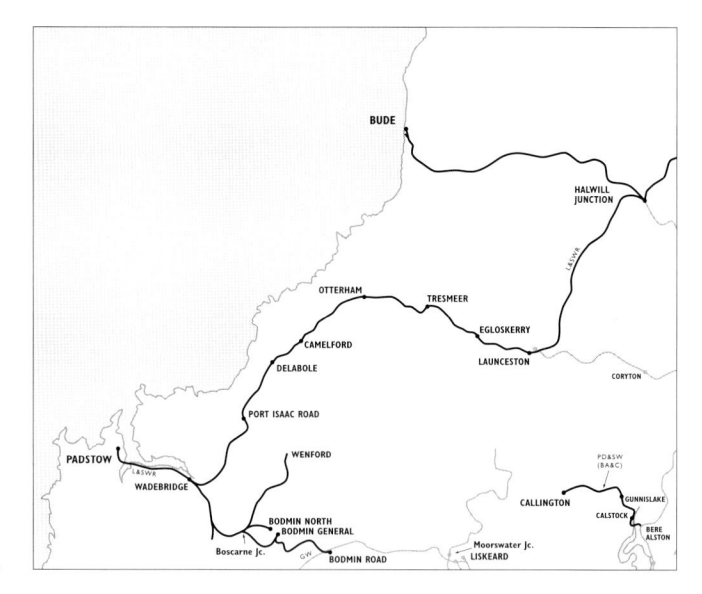

An Ivatt 2-6-2T crossing Calstock Viaduct into Cornwall with a train to Callington. The viaduct was over 100 feet above the valley floor and had twelve 60 foot span main arches, built with concrete blocks cast on site, with construction taking four years. Today, it is promoted in the 'Tamar Valley' publicity as 'The highlight of the journey is when the train slowly creeps down over the Calstock viaduct and you are 120 feet high looking down on the river below. Look closely out of the window and see the National Trust house Cotehele nestled in the woods'.

Ivatt 2-6-2T No. 41315 in the early 1960s at Bere Alston climbing the bank into the station from the Callington Branch. The main line to Plymouth is visible under the bridge on the left. The sixth station out from Plymouth North Road on the former Southern main line to Exeter via North Dartmoor and Okehampton, Bere Alston was the junction for the Callington Branch, running via Calstock and Gunnislake. Bere Alston remains in use today with commuter services from Plymouth to Gunnislake still intact and reversing there, although the main line northwards from Bere Alston to Okehampton was closed in 1968.

CHAPTER 3 - SOUTHERN REGION - CORNWALL

No. 41315 in the 1960s on a freight at Gunnislake was one of the last batch of Crewe-built Class '2' tanks, entering traffic in May 1952 and delivered to the Southern Region. It was at Plymouth Friary from 1953 until that shed closed in May 1963, when it was transferred to Laira for a few months, before moving to Exmouth Junction in September of that year. The line conveyed a large amount of fruit and flower traffic and for many years there were two daily goods trains each way along the branch.

The fashions of the family about to board the train at Gunnislake hauled by No. 41275 give away the date of this picture as early 1960s. Built at Crewe in October 1950, the 2-6-2T spent its first decade on the London Midland Region, alternating between Watford and Bletchley Sheds. It was stored from March until September 1961 and then it was transferred to Plymouth Friary, where it remained until February 1963 when it moved to Wadebridge.

With the extreme edge of West Dartmoor visible on the right, No. 41302 departs from Chilsworthy Halt with a train for Bere Alston in the late 1950s. The village of Chilsworthy was a short distance away down the hill from the Halt. No. 41302 went to the Southern Region at Bricklayers Arms from new in March 1952 and moved to Plymouth Friary in mid-1957; it remained there until that shed closed in May 1963 when it was transferred to Laira.

The Callington Branch had been worked by ex-Plymouth, Devonport & South Western Junction Joint Railway (PD&SWJR) 0-6-2Ts, assisted by 'O2' 0-4-4Ts, until 1953. 'O2' No. 30193 was allocated to Plymouth Friary from mid-1957 until withdrawn in April 1962. Friary duty No. 624 in the summer of 1957 was worked by an 'O2', starting with a passenger service to Bere Alston, after which it spent the morning on the branch before returning to Plymouth. It then went back to Bere Alston and completed another working to Callington where it shunted, later taking a freight to Bere Alston. *Lens of Sutton Association*

Ivatt 2-6-2T No. 41249 at Callington in the early 1960s. It was based at Barnstaple Junction from the end of 1963 and moved to Exmouth Junction in November 1964 after that shed closed; it ended its days on the Somerset & Dorset at Templecombe. The two-road corrugated iron shed at Callington dated from 1908, although it was modified with a new, steeply pitched roof in the 1930s. There was an unusual local practice of berthing coal wagons inside the shed, probably to enable hand coaling to be carried out under cover in this exposed part of the country. This continued even after a coaling stage, which was just out of the picture on the right, had been constructed. *Lens of Sutton Association*

Ivatt 2-6-2T No. 41317 with its smokebox inside the overall roof at Callington on 13th June 1963. No. 41317 was built at Crewe Works in June 1952 for the Southern Region. It went to Eastbourne for a short time before moving to Tunbridge Wells and then Ashford. No. 41317 arrived in the West Country in 1957 based at Plymouth Friary and when that shed closed in May 1963 moved to Laira. Its final shed was Barnstaple Junction in September 1963 and it was withdrawn from there when the shed closed in late 1964. Note the Southern Region style power classification of '2P 2F A' in contrast with the plain '2' on the engines maintained by the London Midland Region. Two of the 2-6-2Ts were sub-shedded at Callington to work the branch from Bere Alston and the last four steam locomotives at Laira were 2-6-2Ts, including No. 41317, retained for the branch until diesel multiple units took over in September 1964. The station was 640 feet above sea level, about a mile north of Callington village, and was actually at Kelly Bray, built on the site of the East Cornwall Mineral Railway depot there. The overall roof was unusual for a branch which had not been built by the Great Western Railway.

Bude

Bude station opened in August 1898 with the arrival of the L&SWR line from Holsworthy, almost twenty years after the line from Halwill Junction to Holsworthy was completed. In the summer of 1958 there were seven weekday stopping trains between Okehampton and Bude, of which one conveyed through coaches from London. There were also two through coaches from the 'Atlantic Coast Express', running non-stop from Exeter St. Davids to Halwill Junction where the Bude and Padstow portions were divided. Summer Saturdays saw more through trains from London, five in 1960 including the 'ACE' and these lasted until June 1963; the line closed in October 1966.

The signal is off but the doors are not yet closed as 'N' Class No. 31831 waits to depart from Bude. The 2-6-0 was one of the large group of the so-called 'Woolworths' which were allocated to Exmouth Junction Shed in the late 1950s and early 1960s. In North Cornwall, the 'Woolworth's were mainly used on freight work, apart from summer specials, until 1961 when they took over the 'T9' turns. No. 31831 left Exmouth Junction in the summer of 1962 for Brighton along with several classmates, No's 31828-30/32-33, when BR Standard 2-6-4Ts displaced by electrification arrived from the South East.
Lens of Sutton Association

Bude station looking toward the buffer stops in the early 1960s. The bay platform held three coaches and an engine; the main platform about seven, ample for the needs of the day. The platform was faced with stone but all other facilities were brick-built. Note the nicely proportioned L&SWR 'barley twist' lamp posts, somewhat spoilt by the fitting of over-height electric fitments.
Lens of Sutton Association

Change was slow coming to branch lines in the South West, even those served by the 'Atlantic Coast Express'. In the mid-sixties Bude station still had its Southern Railway green enamel nameboard. The cars are typical of the 1950s; on the left is a Morris Oxford and to the right is a Ford Anglia 100E, registered in Croydon and very smart in its two-tone paint.
Lens of Sutton Association

CHAPTER 3 - SOUTHERN REGION - CORNWALL

The neighbouring inland town of Stratton was still considered by its residents to be more important, and the station at Bude stopped short of the town centre there to appease Stratton. However, there was a wharf siding extending from near the station, just adjacent to the turntable, across the River Strat on a low bridge whereupon it ran parallel to the Bude Canal. The siding then crossed Vicarage Road, the main road to the west, by this ungated crossing before terminating between the warehouses and the top pond of the canal. Originally it may have extended further to serve the tidal moorings on the River Strat adjacent to the castle. There were no run-round facilities on the siding and only one turnout close to the bridge, so shunting was a lengthy business and involved propelling vehicles from the station yard. Traffic was sufficient to retain the line until at least the early 1960s, as illustrated in these three pictures of 'N' Class No. 31831 on 5th June 1961 showing the 2-6-0 working down the siding.

In the top picture, a German-manufactured Zündapp Bella motor scooter is held up by the shunting manoeuvres. It was one of 130,000 similar machines manufactured between 1953 and 1964 and imported into the UK by Ambassador Motorcycles. The PYN part of the numberplate signified it was registered in central London between March and December 1955. Of course its riders see no need for crash helmets as it only had a 200cc engine generating 10HP, and their elderly appearance suggests they probably have not endured the trip from London on this machine!

Halwill Junction to Padstow

The North Cornwall Railway built the line from Halwill, initially to Launceston between 1884 and 1886, and then in several stages until it reached Wadebridge in 1895, and finally Padstow itself in 1899, after completion of substantial engineering work including the viaduct at Little Petherick and at the terminus itself. Freight services were withdrawn on 7th September 1964 and the last passenger service ran on 1st October 1966. The line from Meldon Junction to Halwill Junction and thence to Wadebridge was closed on 3rd October followed by the Wadebridge to Padstow section on 30th January 1967.

No. 34084 *253 Squadron* arrives at Tresmeer with the 10.35am Waterloo-Padstow on 8th September 1962. The Pacific had moved from Dover to Exmouth Junction in November 1960 and was withdrawn at the end of 1965. Tresmeer was a small village situated about 1½ miles from its station.

Otterham

'N' Class No. 31853 heads for Wadebridge with a mixed freight. It had arrived in the West Country in May 1959 from Bricklayers Arms and worked from Exmouth Junction until withdrawn in mid-1964. There are loaded coal wagons, a pair of cement hoppers and plenty of vans in the 14-wagon train so the revenue might be sufficient to pay the wages on this day! Otterham station platforms and building were still lit by oil lamps, their vessels and burners being stored in the lamp room for use when the nights drew in. Some useful revenue was generated from abroad as this was the local station for U.S. Air Force personnel stationed at Davidstow.

Otterham station, looking towards Wadebridge on 13th June 1961, with a Down freight behind the inevitable Exmouth Junction 'N' Class 2-6-0, in this case No. 31834. Otterham was the most exposed station on the line and was 850 feet above sea level. The station building was in the L&SWR rural style using local Delabole dressed stone. In addition to the usual local agricultural traffic, Otterham was for many years noted for its rabbit trade with crates sent each week to the major cities. *Robert Darlaston*

Wadebridge

'U' Class No. 31635 taking the single token for Padstow as it leaves Wadebridge on 7th August 1956. The Maunsell 2-6-0 was at Exmouth Junction for just over six months, from mid-1956, before moving away to Guildford in January 1957. It had been transferred to the South West from Eastleigh along with classmate, the rebuilt former 'River' Class 'K' 2-6-4T No. 31804, which also left Exmouth Junction on the same date.

'T9' No. 30710 at Wadebridge in the early 1950s was built for the L&SWR in June 1899 by Dübs & Co. It arrived at Exmouth Junction Shed from Salisbury in May 1951 and remained there until withdrawal in April 1959. No. 30710 had been allocated to Wadebridge between February 1937 and February 1940.

Ex-L&SWR Beattie '0298' 2-4-0WT No. 30587 with a short freight at Wadebridge on 7th August 1956. In the background is Wadebridge Shed, which was 115 miles away from Exmouth Junction and therefore had to be relatively self-sufficient; it was provided with a lifting crane, work benches, boiler washout facilities and sand store.

One of the Beattie well tanks was usually employed as the Wadebridge station pilot, and this photograph shows No. 30586 in that role after it had received the later, post-1956, British Railways crest. This engine was frequently to be found on this duty because its water filler was less conveniently placed for taking water in Pencarrow Woods than its two classmates, and so it was rarely used for the Wenford Bridge clay trains, although it was said to be the strongest of the trio and did work the occasional passenger service between Bodmin and Padstow. Wadebridge was originally a terminus, with just one platform road, but was rebuilt in **1888** ready for when the L&SWR (in the guise of the North Cornwall Railway— an independent concern whose services were operated by the L&SWR) finally reached Wadebridge in 1895. It became a through station in 1899 when the extension to Padstow opened, with the facilities increased to three platform faces, a new and larger engine shed and a fifty foot turntable.

Outside-cylinder Pannier tank No. 1368 has replaced the Beattie well tanks on station pilot duties. It is fitted with an 84E Wadebridge shedplate which indicates the picture was taken after September 1963 when the shed's code was changed from 72F. It had arrived there from Weymouth in April 1962 and worked at Wadebridge until withdrawn in October 1964. Note the fireman's shovel jammed into the bunker handrail.

'N' Class 2-6-0 No. 31406, on a train from Padstow, was one of the fifteen engines built in the early 1930s, almost ten years after the majority of the class. They had 'U1'-pattern chimneys and domes, 4,000 gallon tenders with turned-in tops and a step in their footplate. No. 31406 was transferred from Weymouth to Exmouth Junction in February 1962 and was withdrawn from there in September 1964.

'N' Class 2-6-0 No. 31838 in the early 1960s on a Padstow train shows the detail differences of the earlier 'Woolworth' 'N' Class compared to the 1930s batch above, with the flat-topped dome and flat-sided tender especially noticeable.

'57xx' 0-6-0PT No. 4666 on the Molesworth Street level crossing with a train from Padstow. It is still carrying a Danygraig shed plate so this picture was probably taken very soon after its transfer to the South West. The newly-arrived pannier still has BR(W) style lamp brackets, set at 90 degrees to the BR(S) versions, so there must have been some discs configured to suit the different orientation. 4666 went to Exmouth Junction in November 1959, then on to Wadebridge at the end of the year where it remained until February 1963, moving back to Exmouth Junction. The level crossing was situated in the middle of the railway's land, with the station and yards on the east side and the quay lines on the west. It was a constant source of annoyance for motorists because this was the main road leading to the bridge over the River Camel. As can be seen, the line ran adjacent to Eddystone Road, right up against the buildings there. This photograph was taken from the footbridge which would be outside the Co-op supermarket nowadays. The Fish Merchants and King's Fish Cafe is still there today trading as 'Barny's', a fish and chip restaurant and take-away. Just off-picture to the right was Wadebridge West signal box and the fireman prepares to exchange the tablet with the signalman.

CHAPTER 3 - SOUTHERN REGION - CORNWALL

Bulleid 'Battle of Britain' No. 34081 *92 Squadron* with a through train from Waterloo, probably the summer Saturday 'Atlantic Coast Express', in the early 1960s. Built by British Railways in September 1948 and allocated to Ramsgate, No. 34081 was transferred to Exmouth Junction in October 1957. Its final posting was to Eastleigh in July 1964, but it was withdrawn three weeks later. After spending nearly ten years at Woodham Brothers' scrapyard *92 Squadron* was saved for preservation and is currently undergoing repairs after working on various preserved lines from 1998 until 2008, following a 21-year initial restoration.

A handful of passengers cross the footbridge at Wadebridge on 25th June 1962 while a porter brings a barrow to collect the parcels traffic as North British Type '2' No. D6321 waits with a train from Padstow. It is in as-built condition with the two front doors in the nose which opened out to about 160 degrees to allow the flexible gangway connection to be pulled out for multiple working. It would later be fitted with four-character headcode boxes, but remained in green livery until withdrawn in August 1968, with just the addition of small yellow warning panels.

The 7,000th locomotive built at Crewe Works, as evidenced by the commemorative plaques on the tanks below the British Railways crests, No. 41272 with a train for Bodmin on 20th August 1962. The Ivatt 2-6-2T had been transferred to Exmouth Junction in June 1961 and stayed only for two years before moving away to Leamington in July 1963. Note the numberplate on the free-standing concrete bridge, 145 is visible but it is actually 145c, the suffix indicating it is an additional structure added after the line was built and the structures numbered.

On the same day, North British Type '2' No. D6350 arrives at Wadebridge from with a train from Padstow. The wooden footbridge, from which the picture of pannier tank No. 4666 on page 92 was taken, is in the centre background. There is some interesting infrastructure on view, much of it of pure L&SWR origin including lattice and solid post lower quadrant signals, cast iron trespass signs (with the L, &, and W painted out to leave S.R.) and the platform-mounted water column. The Southern Railway added concrete lamp posts and a running-in board made of the same material. Just visible above the impressive coal stack and parked adjacent to the turntable is a 'Birdcage Brake' coach, probably of LB&SCR origin, and in departmental service. No. D6350 contrasts with all these pre-grouping artefacts and had only been delivered from Glasgow in June 1962.

Wadebridge to Padstow

'N' Class 2-6-0 No. 31856 nears Padstow in the early 1960s. It had been transferred to Exmouth Junction in January 1961 from Hither Green. In the background on the left is the 400ft long iron bridge over Little Petherick Creek and on the right the Dennis Hill obelisk, erected in 1889 to celebrate Queen Victoria's 1887 Jubilee.

'N' Class 2-6-0 No. 31838 skirts the Camel estuary near Padstow in the early 1960s.

'T9' 4-4-0 No. 30709 waits to depart from Padstow on 3rd June 1961. Built by Dübs & Co. in June 1899, No. 30709 was a regular at Padstow allocated to Exmouth Junction from 1902, except for six years at Salisbury between 1945 and 1951; it was withdrawn from 72A in July 1961. Padstow was 259 miles and 43 chains from Waterloo. Prominent in the background is the five storey Metropole Hotel which had been opened as the 'South Western Hotel' in 1901 and is still in use today. Rick Stein's super-sized 'chippie' is now where the last two coaches of the train are standing! The station building is still there, complete with fading green paintwork, in the middle of the car park.

'T9' No. 30715 at Padstow on 27th June 1961, relegated to mundane duties just two weeks before withdrawal. Its watercart tender dwarfs the engine. No. 30715 spent its entire working life in the West Country, at Exmouth Junction except for a decade or so at Salisbury in the late 1930s and 1940s.

One of Exmouth Junction's long-serving 'N' Class 2-6-0s, No.31847, at Padstow on 27th June 1961.

'N' Class 2-6-0 No. 31856 waits for departure time at Padstow. It had been transferred to Exmouth Junction in January 1961 from Hither Green and worked from there until withdrawn in July 1964. Padstow had, until the 1960s, extensive fish traffic with a 260ft long fish shed, visible on the right of the picture, and two long sidings extended along the quay.

Bodmin to Wadebridge

The Bodmin & Wadebridge Railway was opened in 1834 and was owned by the London & South Western Railway from 1845. Until the North Cornwall Railway, an independent concern operated by the L&SWR, reached Wadebridge in 1895, the Bodmin and Wadebridge line and its Wenford Bridge Branch remained isolated.

Exmouth Junction 'N' Class No. 31835 passes a pannier in the exchange sidings and heads for Bodmin General at Boscarne Junction around 1963. Photographs of ex-Southern Railway engines at the former GWR station are scarce but as we can see here they did work through. The signal cabin is a standard ex-L&SWR type.

'57xx' No. 4694 in the early 1960s on a local from Padstow to Bodmin North at Boscarne Junction. Another pannier originally allocated to Danygraig, No. 4694 was also transferred to Exmouth Junction in November 1959 and then to Wadebridge a month later. It returned to the Exeter Shed in February 1963 and was withdrawn from there in June 1965.

The guard of a passenger train has just helped a father and toddler off his train and views the photographer somewhat suspiciously. The halt was very basic, being of wooden construction and of tiny proportions. It was graced with three GWR oil lamps and their vessels are stored safely away in a hut. Boscarne Exchange Platform was opened in June 1964, from which date Bodmin North was served by a shuttle railbus from Boscarne, passengers being required to change on or off trains serving Bodmin General. In the background, eleven empty china clay wagons await return to Wenford Clay Sidings.
Lens of Sutton Association

The smallest of the pannier tanks, the six '1366' Class were built in 1934. They had the same short 11ft wheelbase as the '1361' 0-6-0STs, and five of them were first put to use as works shunters at Swindon, the sixth going to Burry Port. When they moved away from Swindon most had spells at Weymouth working in the docks and then in 1962 No's 1367-1369 were sent to Wadebridge to replace the veteran Beattie 2-4-0WTs. No. 1369 had only been there for a few days when it was photographed at Boscarne Junction on a freight from Wenford Bridge on 31st August 1962.

CHAPTER 3 - SOUTHERN REGION - CORNWALL

North British Type '2' No. D6348 at Boscarne Junction with the 2.48pm Bodmin General to Wadebridge on 31st August 1962. It was only a few weeks old, having been delivered from Glasgow in the middle of June. No. D6348 was one of the later locomotives which were built with headcode boxes sunk flush into the aluminium cab frames.

The signal box at Boscarne Junction on 31st August 1962. The purpose of the sidings at the junction was to allow the interchange of china clay traffic from the ex-L&SWR Wenford Bridge line to the GWR route via Bodmin General to Bodmin Road, and thence onto the GWR main line. Two changes in direction were needed, one here and one at Bodmin General. The last freight train between Boscarne Junction and Wadebridge ran on 4th September 1978, although the line remained operational until 31st December.

Bodmin North

Ex-L&SWR 'O2' 0-4-4T No. 30236 in the late 1950s at Bodmin North with a train to Padstow. It was transferred to Wadebridge in December 1955 from Plymouth Friary. No. 30236 was the last 'O2' built, in 1895, and was withdrawn in January 1960. The Wadebridge Shed duty number 606 is painted on the indicator disc and was the Bodmin North passenger service up to 1959, when it became number 646. The station was renamed Bodmin North in 1949. Freight facilities were withdrawn on 24th July 1964, and the station closed on 30th January 1967.
Lens of Sutton Association

The all-pervasive Ivatt 2-6-2Ts had taken over most of the local passenger work in North Devon and Cornwall by 1963. No. 41275 is running around its train at Bodmin North before returning to Wadebridge. It was built by British Railways at Crewe Works in September 1950 and was transferred from the London Midland Region to Plymouth Friary in October 1961, moving to Wadebridge in January 1963. No. 41275 was the regular engine on the Wadebridge service, relieved by a pannier tank when necessary.

The Beattie well tanks and the Wenford Bridge Branch

The Bodmin & Wadebridge Railway was incorporated in 1832 and opened for traffic in 1834. The line from Wadebridge to Bodmin was 6 miles 51 chains whilst the severely curved line to Wenford Bridge, used only for freight and mineral traffic, was 11 miles 63 chains. From Dunmere Junction the latter climbed the valley of the River Camel and for nearly two miles it passed through a beautiful avenue of trees until it reached Penhargard, where the engines stopped to take water from the tank alongside the line.

For sixty years, the Wenford Bridge Branch was the exclusive preserve of three Beattie 2-4-0 well tanks whose survival owed much to their light weight and short wheelbase. They had been built by the L&SWR in the 1870s for suburban work in the south east, but within a decade they had been displaced by larger Adams-designed tank engines and were dispersed to various rural lines around the system. Thirty-one of the eighty-five engines were rebuilt as tender engines with new boilers and six of the remainder were also fitted with similar boilers. Those remaining unrebuilt were withdrawn in the 1890s, along with three of the six reboilered tank engines. Only No's 298, 314 and 329 survived, and this trio eventually ended up at Wadebridge working over the Wenford and Ruthern Bridge Branches of the Bodmin & Wadebridge Railway.

The story actually began with one of the unrebuilt engines which was sent by sea in 1893 from Southampton Docks to Cornwall to work on what was then a remote and isolated section of the L&SWR, unconnected to the rest of the system. Two years later, it was replaced by No. 298, which arrived via the newly completed North Cornwall line which was opened from Halwill to connect Wadebridge with the parent system in June 1895. By 1899 the trio at Wadebridge were the only surviving members of the class, all the others having been withdrawn.

Over the next sixty years, several attempts were made to find more modern replacements for the well tanks but, after trials on the line, none of those selected proved suitable for its sharp curves and low axle loading. The trio continued to work the line and were therefore given new boilers in the 1920s and new front frames and buffer beams in the 1930s, when they were renumbered as No's 3298, 3314 and 3329; under British Railways they became No's 30587, 30585 and 30586 respectively.

Operationally, only one was really needed, the other two being used as a shunter at the awkward-to-operate Wadebridge Quay, shed pilot and 'spare'. The real mystery is why a national railway system could not find suitable replacements until 1962, despite dieselisation of shunting operations since the early 1950s and many small steam shunting engines being displaced. The line was only eleven miles long and mostly freight-only, so line speeds could not have been a problem. Furthermore, all three engines were overhauled at Eastleigh in 1960 and perhaps this merely demonstrated the inefficiencies of a regional railway system where costs were not understood and it was simply easier to accept the 'status quo'. Finally, in September 1962, following a rebuild of the water tank at Pencarrow Woods, they were replaced by three GWR '1366' 0-6-0 pannier tanks which had been displaced from Weymouth, but their reign was short. They were replaced by a 204 bhp diesel-mechanical 0-6-0 shunter but this was underpowered, and a Class '08' diesel shunter operated the line until closure on 26th September 1983.

No. 30587 was selected for preservation as part of the National Collection and, after many years hidden away in the Pullman Works at Preston Park as part of the Reserve Collection, it went on loan to the Dart Valley Railway in April 1978. In December 2001 it was moved to the Flour Mill Workshops in the Forest of Dean for restoration to working order and arrived at Bodmin in November 2002 where it has since remained, apart from a return to the Flour Mill in 2012 for its ten year overhaul, which was completed the following year. The second preserved engine, No. 30585, was purchased privately from British Railways in 1963 for £750 and moved to the Buckinghamshire Railway Centre at Quainton Road in 1969, after spending the intervening years in store at Bishop's Stortford. It was restored to steam in 1970 but was withdrawn in the 1980s when heavy repairs were needed and remained out of use until 2006 when its restoration was completed, also at the Flour Mill Workshops. As part of the restoration terms it has, on several occasions since, spent some time at Bodmin with No. 30587.

No. 30586 at Wadebridge with the Bodmin RU (Restricted Use) GWR 16T 'Toad' brake van on 19th April 1952. The van was branded 'To work between Bodmin, Bodmin Junction and Boscarne Junction', so was only slightly off its designated route. No. 30586 is in an early transitional livery with very small cab numbers and British Railways on the side tanks, both in Southern Railway characters.

No. 30587 acting as shunting pilot at Wadebridge on 7th August 1956; the round topped splashers contrast with those on No. 30586 below. It was built in 1874 at Manchester by Beyer, Peacock & Co. Ltd for the London & South Western Railway and was numbered 298, becoming No. 0298 in June 1898, No. 3298 in 1933 and finally No. 30587 in June 1948 under British Railways. The Wadebridge shunt duty included a trip on the tightly curved quay, this proved problematic for the pannier tank replacements which were restricted to 5mph.

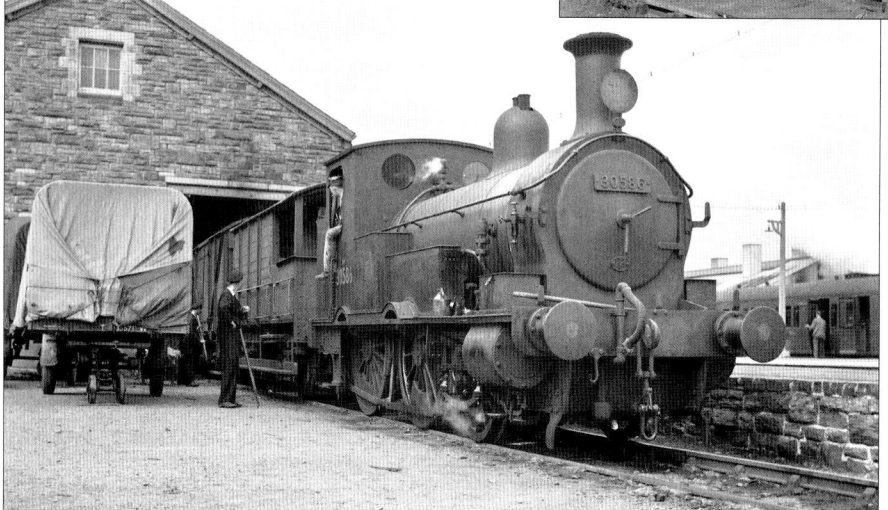

No. 30586 in the oft-photographed pose outside the goods shed at Wadebridge in October 1955. It was the youngest of the trio, being built in 1875, and had square-shaped splashers as opposed to the round ones of the other two engines. It was seldom used on the Wenford Branch because it was awkward to water, as explained on page 104. It was the only one of the three to be scrapped after withdrawal. The 72F Wadebridge shedplate shows up clearly on the smokebox door.

The third member of the trio, No. 30585, basks in the sun at Wadebridge on 19th June 1961. Like No. 30587, it was built in 1874 by Beyer, Peacock & Co. Ltd for the London & South Western Railway and was numbered 314. It became No. 0314 on the duplicate list in 1901, No. 3314 in November 1936 and No. 30585 in December 1948.

No. 30585 at Boscarne Junction sidings with a train of china clay empties for Wenford Bridge on 3rd September 1957. Here china clay traffic was exchanged with the Western Region, there being three sidings; one for fulls, one for empties and one for running round. A Western Region engine would trip the fulls to Bodmin General in rakes of a maximum of nine wagons due to the gradients, returning with empties. From there, they would be taken down to Bodmin Road and the GWR main line.

No. 30585 at Helland Bridge Crossing in the mid-1950s. This was the one of three ungated crossings on the line, but the only one that could justify the guard holding traffic with his red flag; at the others the engine just whistled!

Probably the most photographed water stop in England! No. 30585 at the water tank in Pencarrow Woods on 3rd September 1957. The tank was gravity fed and as can be seen the feed pipe to the locomotive runs almost horizontally. On No. 30586 the water filler in the bunker was taller than on the other two engines, and if it was used on this run it could not be filled and improvisation with buckets was needed. Indeed on one such run in July 1960, when the other two engines were en-route to and from Eastleigh, it took no less than 68 minutes to take water here.

No. 30585 on 5th September 1957 with empties at Pencarrow Woods heading towards Wenford.

No. 30585 in the sidings at Wenford on 3rd September 1957. At Wenford Clay Sidings there was a long loop and four sidings with a goods office. The extensive clay dries were fed by pumped liquified clay of very high quality, mined six miles away at Stannon Moor, and a considerable volume of coal was needed to power the dries, In 1960 about 30,000 tons of powdered clay was produced by the dries, so the line would still have been profitable at this date.

4 – Western Region Mainline – Plymouth to Penzance

West of the Royal Albert Bridge at Saltash, the former broad gauge GWR main line continued its twisting route through Cornwall. There had been many Brunel-built wooden viaducts, but these were all replaced with conventional viaducts by the 1930s as part of the upgrading of the route. As in Devon, the line was a switchback with gradients in both directions, although traffic was lighter and so this was less of an issue. The area around Par and St. Austell was heavily associated with the extraction of china clay, both in solid bulk form and in liquid state and this generated significant revenue for the railways. This traffic was exported from the ports as well as transferred by rail for the pottery and paper industries, some travelling as far as Scotland.

The Royal Albert Bridge and Saltash

'Castle' No. 7001 *Sir James Milne* crossing the single track of Brunel's Royal Albert Bridge with the RCTS 'Brunel Centenarian' from Paddington to Saltash on 2nd May 1959. Pannier tank No. 6420 took over the party there, touring the Plymouth area, including Millbay and Friary, before handing back, appropriately, to 'Castle' No. 5069 *Isambard Kingdom Brunel* for the return journey to London.

Hawksworth 'County' No. 1018 *County of Leicester* crosses the Royal Albert Bridge with a train from Penzance, sometime in the late 1950s and after its allocation to Penzance in November 1954. Note the check rail on the inner rail, and of course there was a permanent speed restriction of 15mph over the bridge.

CHAPTER 4 - WESTERN REGION MAINLINE - PLYMOUTH TO PENZANCE

No. 3686, an '8750' pannier tank, one of the later engines of the '57xx' Class with the Collett cab, working a trip freight through Saltash in the 1950s. It was allocated to Laira from February 1945 until April 1960 when it went north to Chester.

A train of London Midland Region stock runs through Saltash station on 2nd July 1960 hauled by a pair of 'D6300s' which had been in service only since the start of the year. No. D6319 was leading and No. D6310 was the other machine. No. D6319 was unfortunate not to be preserved when it was withdrawn in 1971, but was cut-up after a mix-up between Swindon and Derby, the latter failing to communicate the fact that it had accepted a bid from the late Colin Massingham for the Type '2' which was barely run-in after a General overhaul.

North British Type '2' No. D6325 and a classmate cross into Cornwall over the Royal Albert Bridge on 2nd July 1960. Construction work on the Tamar road bridge, which began in July 1959, is visible in the background.

North British 'Warship' No. D854 *Tiger* runs across Brunel's bridge and into Saltash station with a Cornish-bound trip freight in October 1961, shortly after it entered service. The 83D shed plate on the bufferbeam of No. D854 shows that it is a Laira locomotive. *Tiger* would remain in this original green livery only until the following March when yellow warning panels were applied during its first Light Casual repair at Swindon. On the far hillside, and above the approach to the bridge, there were many United States Marines stationed during World War Two before they made their way down Normandy Hill to the slipways below the bridge for passage to the Normandy beaches in 1944. Plaques affixed to the bridge pillars and a memorial nearby are still there to record this event. Note the GWR 15mph permanent speed restriction sign at the left.

The classic comparison between Brunel's masterpiece and its modern alternative as a 'Warship' heads for Cornwall in the summer of 1961. The Tamar suspension bridge was the longest in the country at the time and opened for traffic in October; The Queen Mother officially opened the bridge on 26th April 1962. Made redundant by the road bridge, the slipway from which the little Saltash vehicle ferry operated is just visible below the main span of the rail bridge.

North British-built 'Warship' No. D862 *Viking* and a classmate cross into Cornwall in the summer of 1962 when the Tamar road bridge was still very quiet – there appears only to be a single coach on it! The train includes several British Railways built Mark 1 coaches still painted in GWR-style 'chocolate and cream'.

'Warship' No. D807 *Caradoc* at Saltash on 8th March 1962 with the afternoon milk train that will have already collected additional fully loaded milk tank wagons as it worked up through Cornwall from Penzance. Although there are tanks standing in the siding, the banner repeater for Saltash's Up Main Starter is off, so it is unlikely it will pick-up any more here. Before dieselisation, the milk tanks were often taken from here up to North Road station on the rear of the Saltash Auto Trains; it is likely that in early DMU days this practice continued. There will be more tanks awaiting the train at Plymouth and particularly at Totnes, where there was an important creamery adjacent to Totnes station, before it reached its destination at Kensington.

Laira's No. 6825 *Llanvair Grange* observes the 15mph speed limit with a westbound freight on 28th April 1962. It was a Penzance engine from February 1946 until July 1962, when it was transferred to Laira. No. 6825 has the later type of tender paired with many of the 'Granges', a Collett 4,000 gallon one. Just visible on the far bank of the Tamar is the Southern Region line to Okehampton and Exeter. The new Tamar road bridge, opened in October 1961, was the first major suspension bridge to be built in the UK after the Second World War.

'Warship' No. D806 *Cambrian* enters Devon with the 12.30pm Penzance to Kensington Milk in 1964. The road bridge is on the right, and below the piers of the rail bridge, over on the Saltash waterfront and in front of the white painted building, is the slipway from where the little car ferry used to berth for its crossing of the Tamar. The ferry ceased to operate when the new road bridge came into use, but the slipways on each side of the river still remain there today. Saltash station lies at the end of the last bridge section, just to the right of the imposing Chapel visible here.

In this picture taken from the road bridge, maroon-liveried 'Warship' No. D828 *Magnificent* takes a westbound freight across the Tamar on 21st August 1967.

The road bridge spoils the distant view somewhat, particularly in comparison with Brunel's Royal Albert Bridge, by which Class '47' No. 1679 has just crossed the Tamar from Cornwall into Devon in May 1972. This picture was taken from a favourite location for the railway photographer, namely the bridge on Normandy Hill. The park on the right is still there today, rather more overgrown than shown here, and the Royal Albert Bridge Signal Box is now used as a store.

With Brunel's bridge clearly silhouetted against the sky a '45xx' 2-6-2T can just be seen crossing the bridge with a short freight in this June 1956 view taken from the trackbed of the Southern Region main line to Okehampton. Ernesettle Jetty in the centre of the picture was connected to the Ministry of Defence depot of the same name by a narrow gauge railway. It was used to re-arm Royal Navy ships.

'Warship' No. D805 *Benbow* runs along the Cornish side of the River Tamar and heads down from Saltash into the Duchy of Cornwall with what looks like a relief to the 'Cornish Riviera' from Paddington. The Royal Navy vessel visible beyond the nearest span of the Royal Albert bridge is alongside the jetty at the Naval Armament Depot at Ernesettle where torpedoes and shells for the warships were stored underground in the facility built deep into the hillside. Live ammunition was not taken on board by the ships or off-loaded here, but would be taken by barge out into Plymouth Sound for loading well away from the City, for safety reasons. *Benbow* carries the headcode '1C35', with the first two characters chalked on and the final two on proper boards slotted into the frames which the first dozen 'Warships' had; it was not fitted with a four-character panel until March 1964.

Menheniot

The pioneer lightweight 'Warship' 2,000bhp diesel-hydraulic based on the German 'V200' design, No. D800 *Sir Brian Robertson* working the 3.20pm Penzance-Paddington after crossing Tresulgan Viaduct, east of Menheniot in the mid-1960s. It was the only one of the class to be withdrawn still in original green livery, in October 1968. A standard headcode box was fitted in March 1964 instead of the steam-style frame No. D800 was built with.

'Western' No. D1055 *Western Advocate* runs through Menheniot station on a P.W. train from Lostwithiel in September 1973, so clearly the headcode displayed is incorrect. No. D1055 came to grief in a collision with a parcels train at Worcester in January 1976 and was immediately withdrawn.

David Burton

Liskeard

Brush Type '4' No. 1935 arrives at Liskeard in the early 1970s with a train to the North East. It was built at the Brush Works in Loughborough in March 1966 and was based on the Western Region until 1986 when it moved to Gateshead. It became No. 47257 in June 1974, 47650 in March 1986 and 47805 in August 1989 and remains in operation to this day.

In addition to being a junction for the Looe Branch, Liskeard was a staging point for china clay traffic as shown here with several rakes of sheeted 'Clayhoods' stored in the Up yard. Birmingham R.C. & W. Co. Class '118' DMU No. W51311 has worked out from Plymouth, the service terminating here. It is in the process of drawing forward out of the long Down platform before reversing over the crossover into the Up platform.

Moorswater

Laira's No. 6849 *Walton Grange* has just passed over the impressive Moorswater viaduct and is starting the climb to Tremabe on a Down train from Plymouth in 1958. It has the 'Intermediate' type of 3,500 gallon tender which was later replaced by the larger 4,000 gallon Collett type.

Bodmin Road

Bodmin Road station looking towards Liskeard in the 1960s. A Down freight has been split as the train engine shunts. The loaded clay wagons to the left are standing on the run-round loop of the Bodmin Branch and have just come down from Wenford via Boscarne Junction. The train engine will add them to this main line train for onward movement to Fowey, a journey that has required a change of direction on three occasions. *Lens of Sutton Association*

The platform staff are ready to load the parcels as No. 4936 *Kinlet Hall* arrives at Bodmin Road with an Up express in September 1955. After withdrawal in January 1964 it languished at Barry Docks until 1981 and it was eventually restored to working order at Tyseley. No. 4936 has since spent a number of years on both main line and preserved railway operation and is currently based at the West Somerset Railway.

In September 1955, one of the very early Churchward '45xx' 2-6-2Ts built in 1907 at Wolverhampton Works, No. 4505 from St. Blazey Shed, waits to depart from Bodmin Road with a 'B-set' on the service to Bodmin General. It just managed to complete fifty years' service before it was withdrawn in October 1957.

'County' 4-6-0 No. 1003 *County of Wilts* departs from Bodmin Road with a Down expresss on 20th August 1962. It had been transferred to Laira in January 1961 after spending the previous decade at Shrewsbury, and was only two months away from withdrawal.

North British 'Warship' No. D844 *Sultan* arrives at Bodmin Road with the 8.30am Paddington-Penzance 'Royal Duchy' on 20th August 1962. It entered traffic in March 1961 and worked for just over ten years, being withdrawn in October 1971.

Lostwithiel

The Churchward '43xx' 2-6-0s were ideal machines for use in Cornwall and were equally at home on both passenger and freight work. No. 5336, which was built in 1917, is on an Up express at Lostwithiel in the mid-1950s. It was allocated to Laira from the end of 1956 until October 1958, except for two months at Bristol St. Philips Marsh in late 1957/early 1958. No. 5336 ended its days at Taunton, working on the Barnstaple line with several other members of the class.

Now 'famous' in red livery as one of the stars in the 'Harry Potter' films, carrying the name *Hogwarts Castle*, No. 5972 in its original guise as *Olton Hall* rolls into Lostwithiel from Bodmin Road with a stopping passenger service on 30th July 1955.

Diesel Multiple Units began to replace the ubiquitous '45xx' 2-6-2Ts in Cornwall in the early 1960s. This is one of the more luxurious Swindon 'Cross Country', later Class '120', units working a Penzance to Plymouth stopping train calling at Lostwithiel on 7th June 1962. In the background, to the right of the goods shed, is the former Cornwall Railway Carriage & Wagon Works.

Robert Darlaston

Par

No. 1018 *County of Leicester* with a westbound express at Par in 1959 while a '45xx' 2-6-2T waits for passengers at the Newquay platform. It had been fitted with a double chimney in January of that year. No. 1018 was allocated to Laira from September 1954 until December 1960.

A rather care-worn 'Warship' No. D862 *Viking* on the 09.30 Paddington to Newquay at Par on a Summer Saturday in 1969. Note the sign for the short-lived Freightliner depot on the left. Par was not a full Freightliner Terminal, but had container stacker machines which placed containers onto the Freightliner flats. The train went to Park Royal in West London, but the service did not last for more than about three years, because the traffic revenue was poor.

St. Austell

A general view of St. Austell in the 1950s, showing the Up and Down platforms and the water tower, looking west as a 'Castle' runs in from Penzance. The Motorail depot was built on the goods yard to the right.
Lens of Sutton Association

Class '52' No. D1043 *Western Duke* at St. Austell heading westwards in the early 1970s. It is not readily apparent from this angle but the signalbox was unusual as it did not have a standard GWR cast iron plate; instead it had a British Railways (W) brown enamel one. The footbridge was originally part of the one which led to St. Austell station and replaced a hazardous level crossing. The roof of the second goods shed, latterly used as a bus depot by Western National, is above the 'Western' on the left.

Brush Type '4' No. 1643 at St. Austell in the early 1970s. This was one of the class built at Crewe Works, entering traffic in January 1965. It became No. 47059 in September 1973, 47631 in November 1985 and 47765 in March 1994, and is now preserved. A diesel shunter is just visible in the background marshalling a train of Carflats and above is a good selection of 1970s cars including an Austin 1800, Austin 1100, Hillman Avenger and Ford Escort together with a Morris Minor and a Mini.

No. D1063 *Western Monitor* assembling its Motorail train at St. Austell. There was a St. Blazey Class '08' shunter out-stabled here, primarily to serve the car unloading facilities, and it would have drawn the loaded Carflats out from the unloading ramps and placed them in the Up platform. The 'Western' would pick up the passenger coaches on the left of the picture, and shunt these to the front of the Carflats before the passengers were loaded, and then depart for London.

Truro

The '4575' 'Small Prairies' were an updated version of Churchward's pre-First World War '45xx' design. A hundred new engines were built in two years between 1927 and 1929. Truro's No. 5515 is ready to depart from Truro with the 11.15am to Falmouth on 21st August 1956. The two-coach 'B-set' has been strengthened by the addition of what looks like a through coach, probably why No. 5515 is not departing from the Falmouth Bay. Alternatively, it could be one of the through trains from Newquay which had to run round at Truro in order to reach their destination.

The 50-year old '45xx' 2-6-2T engines were still in use during the later 1950s. The longest survivor was No. 4508, pictured on shunting duties at Truro on 21st June 1957, which lasted until October 1959. The use of this class is interesting, the task of shunting the yard was normally trusted to one of the shed's powerful '94xx' panniers.

No. 5985 *Mostyn Hall* with a Down parcels at Truro on 8th September 1955. Hawksworth '94xx' 0-6-0PT No. 9434 is in the yard. The 'Hall' was shedded at Truro between May 1953 and January 1956; the Pannier tank went there from new in January 1951 after it was delivered from Robert Stephenson & Hawthorn Ltd's Newcastle works. It worked for just under nine and a half years before being scrapped, and all of its service was in the West Country.

Laira's No. 1010 *County of Caernarvon*, running into Truro with the Paddington-bound 'Cornish Riviera', its headboard devoid of either 'Limited' or 'Express' at this date, although the stock is painted in the 'chocolate and cream' livery introduced in June 1956. The engine will be relieved at Plymouth North Road by the customary 'King' for the onward non-stop run up to the Capital. With their reputation for good hill-climbing, the 'County' Class engines based at Laira and within Cornwall were favourites for such tightly timed workings such as this, and one would often be rostered to the 'Cornish Riviera', working in both directions between Plymouth and Penzance. No. 1010 had moved to Laira from Old Oak Common at the end of 1950 and stayed at the Plymouth shed until October 1959.

No. 1002 *County of Berks*, being turned the hard way at Truro in the mid-1950s, was allocated to Penzance between May 1953 and June 1960; it was fitted with a double chimney at a Heavy General repair in June 1958. Note the GWR cast iron sign attached to a piece of broad gauge 'bridge rail'. These signs are desirable for Railwayana collectors nowadays, their relative scarcity and weight means few have survived.

No. 6837 *Forthampton Grange* arriving at Truro in the mid-1950s. It was shedded at Penzance from November 1952 until May 1960. It may be 'The Cornishman' to us, but to the ladies on the platform it was just a way of getting home! 'The Cornishman' name was first used by the GWR for a Paddington-Penzance service in 1890, but on the introduction of the 'Cornish Riviera Limited' in 1904 the name lapsed; it was revived in 1935 for a summer relief to the 'Limited' until the outbreak of war in 1939. The name was brought back by the Western Region after nationalisation, when it was applied to the daily train from Wolverhampton and Birmingham Snow Hill to Penzance. In 1962, the train was diverted to start from Sheffield and was later extended further north, even starting from Dundee, but the name subsequently fell out of use. Note the GWR-built 'Cornish Riviera Express' Brake Third in the carriage siding.

Penzance-allocated No. 1018 *County of Leicester* piloting a 'Hall' at Truro in 1961. It was at Penzance from December 1960 and has a double chimney fitted in January 1959. The engine shed consisted of three straight roads, shown here being extended, and a taller repair road. The remaining three roads of the building were occupied by the Carriage & Wagon Department.

During their working lives, the engines of the 'County' Class were spread over a wide area of the Western Region but were particularly noted for their work in Cornwall. No. 1006 *County of Cornwall* was fitted with a double chimney in December 1958 while allocated to Penzance Shed but by the time of this picture it had been transferred to Laira, from November 1960. The coaling stage at Truro with its water tank above was a particularly neat design.

Three Hawksworth '94xx' pannier tanks in the shed yard at Truro on 2nd June 1957. In addition to No. 9434 nearest the camera, the photographer recorded No's 8486 and 8412 as being present. They worked the Falmouth Branch passenger trains in addition to their local shunting duties.

With the exception of the stock, a view that has changed very little today, with the station still signalled by British Railways Western Region semaphores and the overgrown yard just retaining a little engineering traffic. A DMU sits in the Falmouth bay platform at Truro in 1962.

North British 'Warship' No. D846 *Steadfast* arriving at Truro with the 09.30 Penzance to London express on 20th September 1965. Its days of front line service on the West of England main line would be over within two years. In June 1967 No. D846 was reallocated to Old Oak Common before going to Tyseley for crew training in preparation for the transfer of over twenty more Class '43s' for use on West Midlands services. They were originally intended for use on the London-Birmingham expresses, but their unreliability saw them quickly relegated mainly to freight and parcels work by the end of November that year.

'Warship' No. D823 *Hermes* with a typical overnight service to the South West, the 00.45 Manchester to Penzance, on Wednesday 29th September 1965. It was in its final year in green livery and was repainted in maroon in mid-1966.

A mix of North British- and Swindon-built 'Warships' heading the Down 'Cornish Riviera' on 24th September 1965, No. D834 *Pathfinder* with No. D818 *Glory* in front. Both would be withdrawn just a few years later with a little over ten years' service, the Class '43' in October 1971 and the Class '42' a year later.

No. D1030 *Western Musketeer* was shunting coaches from the Down to the Up platforms at Truro on 3rd April 1970, only a couple of days after it emerged from Swindon newly repainted in blue with full yellow ends. It was withdrawn on 19th April 1976.

Scorrier

The '45xx' tanks gave sterling service to the Great Western Railway and its Western Region successor. No. 4508, working a local freight at Scorrier on 14th August 1958, had been built at Wolverhampton Works in 1907 and was not withdrawn until October 1959. Scorrier station remained open until October 1964 when it was one of twelve main line stations closed in the Plymouth Division. The total absence of human life in this shot seems to justify that decision.

The 'Granges' were another characteristic class in the Duchy of Cornwall. Also on 14th August 1958, No. 6849 *Walton Grange* runs through Scorrier with a westbound express. No. 6849, which has one of the smaller 3,500 gallon 'Intermediate' tenders, had been transferred to Penzance from Laira during the previous month.

The iconic Cornish image as the Down 'Cornish Riviera Express' powered by No. D1068 *Western Reliance* passes the remains of Hallenbeagle copper mine just east of Scorrier station. The 'Western' had been painted in Rail Blue in April 1970 and was withdrawn in October 1976.

Redruth

The smaller 'Manor' Class were the least numerous of the Great Western mixed traffic 4-6-0s and therefore less common in Cornwall than the 'Halls' and 'Granges'. No. 7806 *Cockington Manor*, on an Up ordinary passenger train east of Redruth in the summer of 1955, was allocated to Truro for only three months before moving away to Machynlleth in October.

Camborne

An early evening scene on the Cornish main line as 'Warship' No. D823 *Hermes* runs through Camborne on 24th August 1963. It is hauling the 6.0pm Penzance-Kensington Olympia 'Milk', but having only picked up from the Unigate sidings at St. Erth, it is still lightly loaded with just six 6-wheel tanks followed by a Hawksworth full brake.

Almost all of the North British Type '2's were originally allocated in the South West, to either Newton Abbot or Laira. Also on 24th August 1963, No. D6310 arrives at Camborne with an Up local service. Built in January 1960, it would receive small yellow warning panels at its next visit to Swindon, but it was never to carry blue livery, being withdrawn in green during March 1971.

Photographed from the footbridge at the eastern end of Camborne station, 'Warship' No. D810 *Cockade* with a Down express on 24th August 1963. It gained the yellow warning panel the previous September and ran in this condition until June 1965, when it went into Swindon Works and was fitted with a standard route indicator panel. No. D810 kept its green livery, albeit adorned with full yellow ends, from early 1968 until repainted in Rail Blue in early 1970.

Gwinear Road

Above: No. 7823 *Hook Norton Manor* with a local service from Penzance at Gwinear Road on 6th June 1957. The Truro-allocated 'Manor' was previously at St. Blazey until the end of 1956; it then made a brief visit to Neath, Wales in summer 1956. It returned to Wales permanently, to Machynlleth in April 1959.

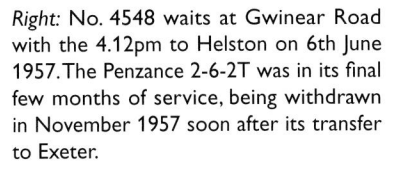

Right: No. 4548 waits at Gwinear Road with the 4.12pm to Helston on 6th June 1957. The Penzance 2-6-2T was in its final few months of service, being withdrawn in November 1957 soon after its transfer to Exeter.

'Castle' No. 7000 *Viscount Portal* has the right away for the main line at Gwinear Road in October 1958. The large running-in board behind which is the Helston platform reads 'GWINEAR ROAD FOR HELSTON, THE LIZARD, MULLION AND PORTHLEVEN'. No. 7000 was built in May 1946 and spent its first decade allocated to Newton Abbot before moving to Gloucester in May 1959. In the strict alphabetical order used by Swindon for its names, No. 7000 should have been called *Cranbrook Castle*, but the name of the man who was to be the last Chairman of the Great Western Railway was applied instead, and No. 7030 took the 'Castle' name.

A pair of North British Type '2's, headed by No. D6308 and followed by No. D6302, arriving at Gwinear Road around the severe curve with an express to Penzance in the early 1960s. The Helston Branch is on the right, running straight on in the distance between the train and the warning sign. At this time Gwinear Road had two signal boxes and in the background is a busy set of sidings including Up and Down loops handling primarily the agricultural produce generated by the Helston Branch and the surrounding area. All this would be removed by the summer of 1965.

Hayle

No. 4966 *Shakenhurst Hall* crosses the distinctive bridge over Copperhouse Pool immediately to the south of Hayle station with a westbound parcels train on 26th July 1953. The first vehicle of the train is a Southern Railway bogie parcels van which is followed by a Great Western outside-framed 'Siphon G'. No. 4966 was at Laira from late 1949 until October 1954 when it was transferred to Neath.

St. Erth

Truro's pride and joy, and the largest locomotive allocated there, 'County' No. 1023 *County of Oxford* arrives at St. Erth with a Penzance-bound express on 7th August 1957.
Lens of Sutton Association

The now-preserved '45xx' 2-6-2T No. 4566 in the St. Ives bay at St. Erth in the late 1950s. Penzance Shed supplied the engines for the branch and No. 4566 was a regular until it was transferred to Laira in September 1961. Plenty of oil cans and cleaning rags are attached to the running plate below the smokebox, no doubt the easiest way for them to be taken to St. Ives Shed.

The large running-in board advises passengers 'ST. ERTH FOR ST. IVES BRANCH' as '45xx' 2-6-2T No.4570 waits in the branch bay platform in the late-1950s. The other large sign further along the Down platform was advertising the British Transport Commission-owned 'Tregenna Castle Hotel', the luxurious hotel owned by the Great Western Railway overlooking St. Ives Bay. It was the name of 'Castle' No. 5006 but was never a real castle, having been built as a luxury residence in the late 18th century. It became a hotel when it was rented by the GWR when the branch opened; the railway purchased it in 1895 and developed it extensively in the late 1920s and early 1930s.

Another 'Small Prairie', No. 4566, waits in the St. Ives Branch bay at St. Erth in the 1950s with a three-coach train, the usual two-coach 'B' set being augmented by a full third. Note the Mediterranean trees on the main line platform supporting the Western's Cornish Riviera publicity!

For many years the 'Small Prairies' handled all the traffic on the St. Ives Branch. The regular engine for many years was No. 4566 which was marshalling the daily freight at St. Erth on 3rd July 1957. The station building on the short platform on the right included a refreshment room that was popular for many years with local farmers who brought their produce to the station for despatch; the siding on which No. 4566 is standing was known by the staff as 'Uncle John'.

North British Type '2' No. D6300 double-heading No. D6304 at St. Erth with a Penzance to Manchester express on 15th September 1959. These were two of the 'Pilot Scheme' batch built in that year and differed in detail from the later production batches; visible in this photograph are the air vents above the cab window and the windscreen wipers mounted below the windows. Both locomotives were withdrawn in May 1968 after less than ten years in service.

'Western' hydraulic No. D1032 *Western Marksman* comes up the 1 in 70 to St. Erth with a westbound express on 2nd April 1970. The St. Ives Branch curves off to the left of the signal box immediately in front of the Western Growers building and their new siding that, unusually, was added as late as 1964, once again indicating the healthy trade in local produce. The Unigate dairy is on the far left of the picture, this being one of the pick-up points for the daily Kensington milk train. No. D1032 was taken out of traffic in January 1973 but was not formally withdrawn until May.

North British Class '43' 'Warship' No. D860, at St. Erth on 2nd April 1970, with an eastbound parcels train and clearly showing the St. Ives Branch accessed via the facing turnout. *Victorious* never carried maroon paint and went straight from green into the blue livery shown here in January 1968.

Marazion

Above: No. 6806 *Blackwell Grange* on an eastbound express runs through Marazion on 27th June 1956. The cattle wagons in the yard are for the extensive brassica, especially broccoli, traffic which originated in this part of Cornwall. No. 6806 was at Hereford until the end of 1955 when it was transferred to Penzance.

Left: Immediately following their introduction, the North British Type '2' diesel-hydraulics were regularly employed in pairs on Type '4' duties in Cornwall. No's D6300 and D6303 pass through Marazion with the 12.0pm Penzance to Paddington on 11th September 1959.

North British 'Warship' No. D834 *Pathfinder* near Marazion with an Up train on 5th January 1970. It went into maroon livery in June 1966, receiving the full yellow ends shown here in February 1968. It was repainted in blue at the end of 1970, only to be withdrawn in October 1971.

Double-headed pairings of 'Westerns' and 'Warships' were quite rare; this is presumably a positioning move for one of these two locomotives. No. D1058 *Western Nobleman* is leading No. D807 *Caradoc* on a Penzance train at Marazion on 6th January 1970; both diesels are in Rail Blue.

CHAPTER 4 - WESTERN REGION MAINLINE - PLYMOUTH TO PENZANCE

Penzance

It is raining outside as a young lad takes in the pleasures of Penzance station on 19th April 1952. If the Platform 1 number is anything to go by, the station signage is still pure GWR, as are the lamps hanging from the roof. The three main platforms are all occupied by ex-GWR coaches, the products of Collett and Hawksworth, although there may be a 'Toplight' vehicle from the turn of the century as part of the train in Platform 1. None of the coach destination boards are readable so they may well be turned over onto their blank sides, and note the grill protecting the glass on the droplight of the Brake Third, a standard GWR fitting. Outside the station roof, the Royal Mail train is parked in its usual position but there is not an engine to be seen anywhere – let's hope our lad did not get too wet looking for one!

Laira's No. 1015 *County of Gloucester* runs into Penzance on 3rd September 1956 with the down 'Cornish Riviera', the 10.30am from Paddington, which this engine will have taken over at Plymouth. Saint Michael's Mount is just visible in the background, and the large boulders on the right are sea defences for the line at this point which is close to the waters in Mounts Bay. The Running Foremen at Laira would often use a 'County' on this working, the locomotive being quite likely to work back from Penzance to Plymouth the following day on the up 'Riviera' or possibly on the Kensington milk train.

No. 4959 *Purley Hall*, a Bristol Bath Road-allocated engine, photographed from the road overlooking Penzance station on 3rd September 1956. It was normal operating procedure for an arriving engine to back out its rake of coaching stock to the carriage sidings at Long Rock for cleaning and maintenance; the depot can be seen in the distance.

CHAPTER 4 - WESTERN REGION MAINLINE - PLYMOUTH TO PENZANCE

Churchward 2-6-0 No. 7316 from Exeter in the shed yard at Penzance on 3rd September 1956, has been turned and is now facing in the right direction for a return back home via Truro and Plymouth, almost certainly on a freight.

No. 6808 *Beenham Grange* in unlined black alongside Hall No. 5972 *Olton Hall* on Penzance Shed in the early 1950s. New in October 1936, No. 6808 was allocated to several depots in Devon and Cornwall until it was transferred from Penzance to Cardiff East Dock in September 1962, when Penzance Shed officially closed to steam. The building dated from 1914 and was a standard Great Western Railway design with four roads, each capable of holding three tender locomotives, and a Lifting Shop. Penzance had nine 'Halls' and ten 'Granges' in the mid-1950s and these rarely ventured east of Plymouth.

'Modified Hall' No. 6988 *Swithland Hall* ready to depart from Penzance with 'The Cornishman' on 27th June 1956. The 'Halls' were often used on express passenger duties such as this in Cornwall. No. 6988 was built under British Railways auspices in March 1948. The updated design introduced by Hawksworth in 1944 incorporated a larger superheater, new pattern cylinders, smokebox saddle and frame details and a longer wheelbase bogie with plate frames and stretcher. From No. 6971 onwards they were paired with the straight-sided pattern of tender.

No. 9463, with a shunter in nicely washed overalls posing on his shunters' truck, at the carriage sidings at Long Rock on 3rd September 1956. In the background, the Travelling Post Office stock waits in the distance ready for the overnight working to Bristol and beyond.

It is all quiet at the end of the line in this view with Hawksworth '94xx' 0-6-0PT No. 9463 acting as station pilot and marshalling stock on the left, and a number of carriage sets in the platforms. Although relatively sheltered from the sea by Mounts Bay, there was still a need for substantial protection for the station and its tracks when the winter storms blew in from the west, hence the massive boulders visible on the seaward side of the boundary wall. No. 9463 was built at the Newcastle Works of Robert Stephenson & Hawthorns Ltd in January 1952 and except for a month at Newton Abbot spent its first six years at Penzance along with No. 9462. Its short working life ended in June 1965 when it was withdrawn from Southall.

Penzance Shed faced east and all locomotives were turned after coaling. On 2nd June 1957 local 'Hall' No. 4931 *Hanbury Hall* keeps company with a pair of unidentified 'Counties', a '43xx' 2-6-0 and another 'Hall'. On the right there is a 4,000 gallon Collett tender coaled up, but separated from its engine; it will have come off either a 'Castle', 'Hall' or 'Grange'. The repair road is that on the extreme right with the Boiler and Pump Houses in front, so the engine to which it belongs is most probably in there.

The first 'Grange', No 6800 *Arlington Grange*, was allocated to Penzance from the end of 1953 until July 1962. It is standing outside the depot, known to railwaymen as Long Rock, on January 14th 1962. No. 6800 looks fresh from overhaul, but records show its last works attention was a Heavy General at Swindon in March 1960. It is coupled to Collett 4,000 gallon tender No.2537, which it was paired with from May 1960, and is complete with overhead electrification warning flashes – something that would only be appropriate if it made it as far north as Crewe! The 'Granges' may have been a replacement for Churchward '43xx' 2-6-0s but only the wheels, rods and cab steps, plus the re-used tenders, survived the 'accountants re-building'.

Above: 'Warship' No. D810 *Cockade* after arrival at Penzance with a Down express in 1961. It did not receive yellow warning panels until September 1962 and a standard route indicator panel until June 1965.

Left: North British Type '2' No. D6312 is acting as station pilot at Penzance station in late 1963 or early 1964. The shunter is just climbing off the shunters' truck and will be coupling up the rake of Southern Region coaches that have just arrived.

Left: 'Warship' No. D819 *Goliath* backing out of Penzance station on 13th June 1965 after arriving with the Down 'Cornish Riviera'; the time-honoured 10.30 from Paddington.

Below: A pair of multiple-working-fitted 'Warships' of Class '42', No. D866 *Zebra* and No. D823 *Hermes* prepare to depart from Penzance with the 10.15 'Cornish Riviera Express' to Paddington on a miserable July day in 1968. The paintwork on both locomotives is in very poor condition; *Zebra* is in green and *Hermes* is in maroon. They are pulling mostly blue and grey-liveried stock forming the Western Region's most prestigious train in the age of British Rail's new 'Corporate Image'!

CHAPTER 4 - WESTERN REGION MAINLINE - PLYMOUTH TO PENZANCE

'Warship' No. D809 *Champion* on a summer Saturday in July 1968 passing Long Rock Depot with the 3A97 15.40 Penzance-Paddington perishables. This was the 19.20 ex-Plymouth on every other day of the week, and was booked for two Class '42's. No. D809 was repainted in maroon with a small yellow warning panel in March 1966, the full yellow ends being applied two years later.

No. D831 *Monarch* running light-engine on the up main line near Ponsandane Signal Box, again in July 1968. On 30th November 1966 *Monarch* had been the second 'Warship' to emerge from Swindon in the new Rail Blue. These first repaints were supposed to have 6in. 'D'-prefixed numbers in the new Rail Alphabet, immediately behind the cab door, and double-arrow symbols on the cab sides, but instead Swindon used old pattern serif numbers underneath the bodyside windows in line with the double arrow symbols on each cab. Unlike the first repaint, No. D864 *Zambesi*, which had the prescribed full yellow ends, *Monarch* had for some reason reverted back to small yellow warning panels. It eventually received the standard Corporate Blue in March 1969 and was withdrawn in October 1971.

Blue-liveried 'Warship' No. D814 *Dragon* is signalled away from Penzance in July 1968. It had been repainted in blue with full yellow ends, double insignia, serif numbers, and with 'D'-prefix in August 1967. This lasted until its final livery change in May 1969, when it gained the later sans-serif numerals and lost its 'D'-prefix. *Dragon* has the multiple-working equipment which was refitted for the double-headed workings in 1968. It was withdrawn at the end of 1971, but was one of three Class '42's reinstated in March 1972. It is displaying the 3A67 headcode which was for the 16.55 St. Erth-Kensington Milk train, and it is likely that No. D814 had worked this on the previous day as far as Plymouth, and then worked back down to Penzance overnight.

'Warships' No's D861 *Vigilant* and 868 *Zephyr* have arrived at the end of the line at Penzance on 21st June 1970. A total of 4,400 brake horsepower was somewhat excessive for a six-coach stopping passenger train, and this was probably a positioning working to bring one of the two locomotives from Laira using a single crew and taking up one less timetable path. No. 868 never carried maroon livery and was in its first style of blue with full yellow ends, with two double arrows, serif numbers and 'D'-prefix, whereas No. D861 is still in maroon with a small yellow warning panel, which it had from September 1966 until repainted blue in March 1971. Both locomotives were withdrawn in the great cull of hydraulics in October 1971 when twenty-nine 'Warships' were taken out of service. Note that some of the GWR 'art deco' lamp shades in the 1952 station view (page 145) are still in place nearly twenty years later, although the end screen, evident in the earlier photograph, has been removed.

CHAPTER 4 - WESTERN REGION MAINLINE - PLYMOUTH TO PENZANCE

Time has moved on and the 'Warships' have been withdrawn. 'Westerns' now have a near monopoly on the Cornish main line. No. D1051 *Western Ambassador* is backing out of Penzance having brought in an express from Paddington. However, paint standards are still poor and it is definitely not a good ambassador for the 'Corporate Image'. The cleaning chemicals used by the Western Region in its carriage washing plants were very harmful for the train engines that took the rakes through, and this caused premature paint wear.

Another 'Thousander', as the crews called them, stands at Long Rock Depot between duties in 1973. No. D1001 *Western Pathfinder* is in much better external condition than No. D1051. One of the authors remembers creeping around this depot as a spotter during this period around 3am one summer morning. Unsurprisingly, it was completely unattended. There was no artificial light and the place remained unchanged since its days as a steam shed. There was even an old steam tender outside in the yard.

With the withdrawal of steam there was no need for 'D'-prefixed locomotive numbers. These were easily dropped on other Regions on re-painting, when the 'D' was simply not re-applied. However, in true GWR style, Swindon had put cast numberplates on its 'Westerns'. Although the 'D' and the numerals were screwed to a steel backplate, no attempt was made to remove the 'D', it was simply painted over as shown on No. D1001 *Western Pathfinder* as it waits to depart for Paddington in 1973.

5 – Western Region Cornish branch lines

Cornish branch lines fell into two categories, those that struck off from the main line to the coast, and those that serviced the china clay industry. The central area north of St. Austell was a harsh barren environment dominated by slag heaps and clay pits. The Par to Newquay Branch was by far the most important, with a foot in both camps. There was specialisation too, with the Fowey Branch serving a deep sea china clay port and Falmouth an important dockyard. However, it is for holiday traffic that most will remember the branches, powered by their '14xx' and 'Prairie' tank engines.

Looe

'4575' 2-6-2T No. 5557 and 'B-set' wait at Liskeard with a train from Looe in the late 1950s. The branch platform here was unusually positioned at ninety degrees to the main platforms, a feature dictated by the topography of the land and no doubt a need to keep construction costs down. No. 5557 had been transferred from Newton Abbot to St. Blazey in October 1955, staying there until withdrawn in October 1960. This is an interesting view of two of the once common GWR waiting room benches – made to last, but not be exposed to outside elements, as they are here.

'Small Prairie' No. 5557 had arrived at Liskeard from Looe on 18th April 1960 and prepares to back its 'B-set' stock up to the run-round loop.

Once the DMUs had arrived and proved themselves, there was no need for the run-round loop at Liskeard and it was removed. A DMU waits in the Looe platform in the mid-1960s.

No. 5502 at Coombe Junction near Liskeard on 8th September 1955. The St. Blazey-allocated '4575' was one of the earliest to be withdrawn, in July 1958. Coombe Junction was the only passing place on the branch and operation was complicated by the need for all trains to reverse. The first train to arrive ran directly into the platform, then the engine ran round its train and shunted it into the loop to allow the second train to enter the platform. Moorswater Viaduct on the Cornish main line can be discerned in the distance.

'45xx' No. 4565 coming down the incline from Liskeard to Coombe Junction on 18th August 1959. After running around the train it will take the line to Looe on the right. The lined green 2-6-2T had been allocated to St. Blazey since 1941 and was withdrawn from there in October 1961.

The last of the '45xx' 2-6-2Ts, No. 4574, running through the countryside near Causeland on 30th May 1961.

'45xx' No. 4552 approaching Looe on 5th August 1956. St. Blazey Shed provided the motive power for the branch and No. 4552 stayed there until withdrawn in September 1961.

No. 4574 at the end of the line in 1961. Unlike several of the other St. Blazey 2-6-2Ts, it was not withdrawn there, but moved away to Newton Abbot in September 1961. Note the very large decorative rock and floral sign in the ground on the left spelling out 'LOOE'. Unfortunately, it was more visible to passengers awaiting their train than those arriving.

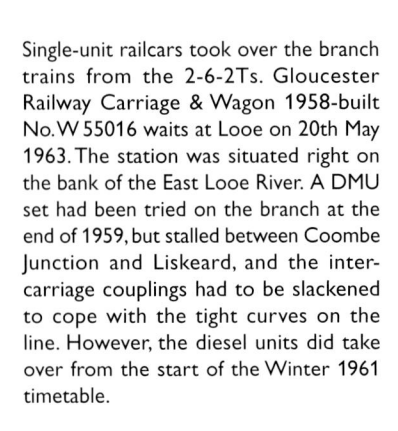

Single-unit railcars took over the branch trains from the 2-6-2Ts. Gloucester Railway Carriage & Wagon 1958-built No. W 55016 waits at Looe on 20th May 1963. The station was situated right on the bank of the East Looe River. A DMU set had been tried on the branch at the end of 1959, but stalled between Coombe Junction and Liskeard, and the inter-carriage couplings had to be slackened to cope with the tight curves on the line. However, the diesel units did take over from the start of the Winter 1961 timetable.

CHAPTER 5 - WESTERN REGION CORNISH BRANCH LINES

Bodmin and Wadebridge

Right: '4575' 2-6-2T No. 5521 with the obligatory 'B-set' at Bodmin Road on 10th May 1958. It was nearing the end of its stay in Cornwall, leaving in August for Taunton. This station boasted two water tanks, and the one visible in the distance had an unusual cantilevered gantry arrangement to bring the water over the branch tracks to a hanging column on the Up platform.

Below: St. Blazey-allocated '45xx' No. 4552 leaving the terminus at Bodmin General bunker-first is heading for Bodmin Road on 2nd June 1960. The service had been worked by 'Prairie' tanks since the late 1920s and all engines on this line faced 'chimney towards Bodmin General', due to the 1 in 37 incline. Note the single track engine shed above the train, and the branch from Boscarne Junction, where china clay traffic was exchanged from the Wenford Bridge line, coming in on the left after the yard and loop turnout. This made for operational complications because the majority of traffic, bound for Bodmin Road, came up the branch in short trains but would depart downhill in longer freights.

'4575' 2-6-2T No. 5519 at Wadebridge on a train to Bodmin, which was around seven miles away, in the 1950s. Several GWR passenger trains had been extended to Wadebridge SR in the 1930s, but after nationalisation in 1948 some were extended further to operate from Bodmin Road to Padstow via Bodmin General and Wadebridge. All this, of course, was not good news for the ex-Southern Railway station at Bodmin North which was almost 'surplus to requirements'. The 1927-built No. 5519 was withdrawn in June 1960. It was at St. Blazey throughout the 1950s until mid-1959 when it was transferred to Laira.

A St. Blazey '45xx' No. 4569 after arrival at Wadebridge on 27th July 1960 with the 12.20pm from Bodmin Road.

A typical run-down branch line scene of the mid-1960s, with an expensive new diesel and a single Stanier coach arriving at Bodmin General from Wadebridge. North British 'Type 2' No. D6317 is one of the earlier locomotives which were retro-fitted with headcode boxes; these were accommodated by slicing the two gangway doors vertically to fold back on themselves so they did not foul the boxes when opened. The passenger service ceased in January 1967, with three coaches behind the Type '2' to accommodate those who wanted to make what they thought would be their final journey on the line on 28th January. The line lingered on due to the china clay traffic as freight only just long enough to be taken over by the preservation society and today it is a lovely thriving railway full of character and well worth a visit.

North British Type '2' No. D6306 has arrived at Bodmin General in the pouring rain with the train from Bodmin Road. The early 1960s mail traffic looks very healthy so it may be near Christmas – the weather certainly fits! Another locomotive of the same class is visible in the distance and since this has a small yellow warning panel the date is probably late 1962. This other Type '2' is on the same track and so will back onto the train and take it to Wadebridge. These small diesel-hydraulics seemed to replace steam on a 'one-for-one' basis on many branch lines, so the working practices from steam days continued.

Fowey

The Fowey Branch was a loop leaving the main line at Lostwithiel, extending down to Fowey where there were extensive china clay ship loading facilities, before looping back up to St. Blazey which was on the Newquay line just after Par station. Although a passenger service shuffled between Lostwithiel and Fowey, china clay traffic was the reason for the existence of the branch. This came from both directions, directly from the mines on the Newquay Branch around Bugle and Roche to Fowey, from Wenford via Bodmin Road, and from the branches joining the main line at Burngullow west of St. Austell. All of this traffic would travel along the main line to Lostwithiel and arrive at Fowey from that direction. The line between Par and Fowey was sold to English China Clays in 1968 and converted into a private road with tipper trucks operating along it, but the section from Lostwithiel to the Fowey loading jetties at Carne Point remains open for carrying china clay by train.

'14xx' 0-4-2T No. 1419 waits patiently in the Fowey Branch platform at Lostwithiel in the early 1950s. The driver takes a break on the GWR bench – it could have been placed there especially for him!

No. 1419 arriving at Fowey with its Auto Trailer in July 1955. Nicknamed 'Maud', this auto-fitted '14xx' was allocated to St. Blazey, and apart from works visits, was a fixture on the Lostwithiel to Fowey service for many years. A Gloucester Railway Carriage & Wagon Co. single car diesel unit took over the service on 17th April 1961.

CHAPTER 5 - WESTERN REGION CORNISH BRANCH LINES

According to the milepost, it is a full 286 miles and 20 chains from Paddington, as No. 1419 stands ready to propel its auto-coach out of the platform at Fowey. Although the starter signal is off and the route indicator is set for the Up Main, there is still plenty of activity on the platform so departure is not imminent. The passenger service was withdrawn in March 1964, although the branch remained open for the large volume of china clay traffic.

1924-built '45xx' 2-6-2T No. 4569 arriving at Fowey, probably in 1960, was a long-standing St. Blazey engine, from November 1948 until July 1961 when it went to Whitland in South Wales. It is resplendent in the lined green livery which Swindon Works applied to a large number of engines which had been painted black in the early days of British Railways, once the Western Region was let off the leash in the mid-1950s.

Above: An unidentified '42xx' 2-8-0T arrives with another load of china clay for the jetties as the branch '14xx' 0-4-2T simmers out of the way in the bay platform at Fowey. A timeless scene taken in the early 1960s, but it could have been taken at any time since the 1930s.
Lens of Sutton Association

Left: The last in a long line of pannier tank designs from Swindon, the small '16xx' were all built by British Railways from 1949 to 1955. They were effectively an updated version of the old '2021' 0-6-0PTs and even had the same wheel diameter. A large number went to Wales to replace a plethora of antiques, many of which dated back to the 19th century. No. 1624 arrived at St. Blazey in October 1953 after three months at Laira, following its departure from Machynlleth in July. It is pictured shunting at Fowey in July 1955 and stayed in Cornwall until the end of its days, in February 1962.

CHAPTER 5 - WESTERN REGION CORNISH BRANCH LINES

Left: '45xx' No. 4552 resting at Fowey in July 1955 with 2-8-0T No. 4206. The 'Small Prairie', like most of the engines working on the branch, was from St. Blazey Shed and No. 4552 stayed there until withdrawn in September 1961.

Below:
The powerful Churchward '42xx' 2-8-0Ts were the staple power for the china clay trains which ran on the Fowey Branch and two were allocated for this purpose to St. Blazey for many years. No. 4206 working a train of empty china clay wagons in July 1955 was one of the oldest in the class, dating from 1912 and was withdrawn in December 1959.

No. 4206 drags the chalk-stained empties through the platform at Fowey. The wooden bodied 'clay-hood' wagons were some of the last examples of the traditional British four-wheeled open wagon, working until around 1988. The wagons are branded 'FOR CHINA CLAY TRAFFIC ONLY - EMPTY TO ST BLAZEY WR'.

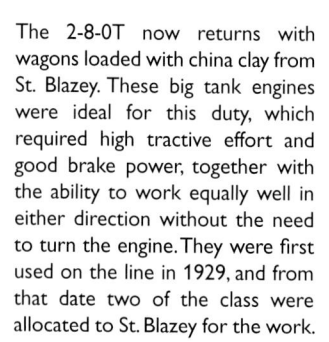

The 2-8-0T now returns with wagons loaded with china clay from St. Blazey. These big tank engines were ideal for this duty, which required high tractive effort and good brake power, together with the ability to work equally well in either direction without the need to turn the engine. They were first used on the line in 1929, and from that date two of the class were allocated to St. Blazey for the work.

No. 4206 now has a full load of white-stained tarpaulin-covered clay wagons as it approaches Fowey from Par. Along with No. 4247, it worked these trains in the mid-1950s, the latter leaving for South Wales in January 1958 and eventual preservation via Woodham Brothers' Barry scrapyard, but No. 4206 stayed until withdrawal in December 1959. The ringed signal arms indicate this is a goods-only line, the passenger service between Fowey and Par having ceased in 1929.

'Warship' No. D838 *Rapid* on a china clay trip working passes what was then the wagon works at St. Blazey. It went into traffic at Laira in October 1960 and was transferred to Newton Abbot in November 1961, where it remained until October 1967, when most of the North British built members of the class were concentrated at Old Oak Common. *Rapid* is in its original condition; overhead warning plates were added in September 1961 and yellow warning panels in May 1962; it was repainted in maroon in 1966 and blue in 1968. Note the steam style 83D Laira shedplate on the buffer beam and the North British diamond-shaped maker's plate on the solebar, directly below the nameplate. No. D838 was withdrawn in March 1971 after just over ten years' service with a recorded mileage of 715,000.

CHAPTER 5 - WESTERN REGION CORNISH BRANCH LINES

Rail Blue Class '22's No. 6326 and No. D6333 at the south end of St. Blazey Shed in around 1969. No. D6333 is in an earlier blue livery variant with serif 'D'-prefixed numbers above the double arrow whereas No. 6326 is in the final version using the newer sans-serif Rail Alphabet numbers below the emblem. The bridge in the background carries the Western Region main line over the lines to Par Harbour and Fowey.

Class '25' No. 7624 being turned by hand at St. Blazey Shed in September 1973. As the only way to access the maintenance facilities was via the turntable, there was no alternative to manual operation of the table when the vacuum gear on the turntable or locomotive was faulty. No. 7624 was originally an Eastern Region machine, moving to the Western at Newport Ebbw Junction in late 1970 before transfer to Laira two years later. It moved again the month after this picture was taken, to Bristol Bath Road, before ending its days at Bescot; it became No. 25274 under TOPS and was withdrawn in May 1982.

Parkandillack

'4575' 2-6-2T No. 5519 is passing Dubbers Siding and clay drying kiln, on the left, between Drinnick and Treviscoe on the Parkandillack Branch, which left the main line at Burngullow. The roof of Drinnick Mill goods station can just be made out above the roofs of the two sheeted vans. The mineral wagons at the front of the train may contain coal for Treviscoe, whilst the vans are almost certainly empties being taken down to Kernick or bound for the Retew Branch, to be loaded with bagged clay (if the train was loaded it would have merited a second locomotive). The line to Drinnick branched off to the left just behind the brake van, dropping down to a run round and buffer stops; it then ran back beneath the train (the bridge is just visible around the centre point of the train) to reach Drinnick Dryers. No. 5519's train is divided – there is a gap in the rake of vans before the ones that are sheeted over. The loop and signal box were still in use at this time so some vehicles must be in the process of being dropped off/collected via the loop, as Drinnick Mill and Dubbers siding could only be shunted in the opposite direction and this could be for No. 5519's return trip. No. 5519 was at St. Blazey from June 1946 until July 1959 when t was transferred to Laira.

CHAPTER 5 - WESTERN REGION CORNISH BRANCH LINES

Pannier tank No. 9673 is double-heading with another '4575' past Little Treviscoe Siding, with loaded wagons from Drinnick or Goonvean. Loaded trains ran out via St. Dennis and then along the Newquay Branch (this would also apply to the wagons behind No. 5519 on the previous page, once they had been loaded). No. 9673 was a regular performer as the Drinnick pilot at this period. It went new to Laira in February 1949 and moved to St. Blazey in March 1951, from where it was withdrawn in May 1960.

The Newquay Branches

The important holiday town of Newquay was reached by two branches off the Cornish main line. Principal services came from the north via Par through the 'Cornish Alps', which were spoil heaps from china clay mining, so this was not a totally picturesque route and was sparsely populated. The other route was from a junction at Chacewater, west of Truro, which faced the Plymouth direction, although this was a triangle until 1919. This branch was much prettier, with more stations, but traffic was still very local and of low volume. The Par line carried significant china clay traffic and it would be this one that survived.

Luxulyan

'4575' No. 4587 on a wet day at Luxulyan in the late 1950s. It had been in Cornwall since October 1953, moving to Truro in July 1954 and finally St. Blazey in December 1958, from where it was withdrawn in July 1960. Note Camping Coach No. W 9906 W on the right.

Newquay

'57xx' 0-6-0PT No. 7715 at Newquay in July 1955. It was built for the GWR by Kerr, Stuart & Co. in May 1930 under one of the Government schemes to alleviate the effects of the post-1929 depression. No. 7715 was, at the time, one of only two panniers with the older style cab based in Cornwall and spent most of its life allocated to St. Blazey, with short spells at Newton Abbot and Laira before moving to a South Wales shed, Duffryn Yard, in January 1962.

CHAPTER 5 - WESTERN REGION CORNISH BRANCH LINES

The fireman is moving the lamp from the centre bottom bracket (indicating Light Engine) to the upper bracket (indicating Branch Passenger Train) of Truro Shed's '4575' 2-6-2T No. 5562 at Newquay on 16th August 1959, before it can depart with the 10.50am to Falmouth. The interesting building on the right was the town gas works which, despite its position, was never rail connected.

A pair of Gloucester R.C. & W. single car DMUs running together on the service to Par stand at Newquay in around 1962. The station had three long platforms and the freight facilities were once quite extensive, but were closed in 1965 leaving four carriage sidings. They did not last long and these too were all lifted by 1969. The Chacewater to Newquay Branch line closed in February 1963.

Perranporth

Perranporth on 7th June 1962 with the 2.58pm Truro to Newquay service operated by a single-unit railcar. Note the 'Public Notice' of forthcoming closure. The upper shot is looking towards Newquay and the lower one towards St.Agnes. *Both Robert Darlaston*

A characteristic Great Western 'pagoda' hut served as the station building at Mithian Halt between Perranporth and St.Agnes. No. 5515's 'B-set' looks quite full as it departs from there on 14th August 1958.

Two youngsters lean over the bridge parapet to watch No. D6324 arrive at St.Agnes with a local trip freight from Newquay on 15th August 1962. The Type '2' had already been fitted with the first pattern of headcode boxes, which were bulky and poorly designed, letting in water and rusting so that the mechanism inside jammed. They were replaced on No. D6324 in 1966 by an improved design mounted flush with the cab front, which was used on all except a couple of the earlier locomotives built without headcode boxes.

A Birmingham Railway Carriage & Wagon Company three-car DMU, running with its centre car removed, forms the 3.30pm to Newquay at St.Agnes on 15th August 1962. The trailing car is No. W51314. There were ten stations or halts on the 18½ mile Chacewater to Newquay Branch line, but only St.Agnes, Perranporth and Shepherds & Treamble had passing loops.

At Chacewater, No. 4593 heads an interesting pair of coaches on a train bound for Truro; the first is a recently repainted Collett 70ft Third Class flat ended coach (i.e. before they moved to bow-ended) to Diagram C46 lot 1337 built in 1925, running No. 4734. The second coach is, we think, a Hawksworth 60ft Brake Third to Diagram D133 built in 1949. Originally, it was thought to be a 1938 vehicle to Diagram D127 but the position of the name board brackets is different and the ends in the photograph appear to be domed, so D133 is most likely. The cast '37' on the end of No. 4734 is the tare weight, the average for that lot being 36t-10c-1q. The '4575' operated from Truro Shed between January 1960 and September 1961, leaving for Taunton.

Falmouth

The Falmouth Branch was 11¾ miles long, with three intermediate stations and a short freight spur to Newham Wharf on the outskirts of Truro. Opened in 1863, with the connection to the commercial docks opened one year later, there had been great hopes for substantial traffic in china clay, but the deep water Fowey Docks were both better placed and equipped. However, Falmouth Docks was still an important port for ship repair, especially after the graving docks were commissioned.

No. 4549 had lost its smokebox number plate and has had a Great Western style replacement painted onto the bufferbeam. The '45xx' was in its final year of service when photographed arriving at Perranwell, the first station out of Truro, with a Falmouth bound train on 29th May 1961.

Falmouth station was still blessed with the protection of this Brunel-designed overall roof in the early 1950s, but it had been removed by 1959. For those interested in such things, the parcels vehicle is an LM&SR Period 1 passenger brake to diagram D1778. It has lost some of its original beading as the plywood has been plated over, a common feature in post-war LM&SR or BR days, and seldom modelled. *Lens of Sutton Association*

Two dock cranes form the backdrop for this view of Falmouth station on 15th August 1959, the line to the docks descending down beyond the station building on the left. '4575' 2-6-2T No. 5559 had six months left in service and was withdrawn from Truro in January 1960. The large poster on the right states that you could 'Save 4/- in the £ on your 2nd class rail fare by travelling mid-week'. The unusual left-hand drive split-screen vehicle parked on the right is an American 1941 Dodge D19 'Luxury Liner' two-door coupé with 'Fluid Drive' transmission, probably left over from the war when Falmouth and the surrounding areas were home to many thousands of US servicemen preparing for the Normandy landings.

Contrasting with the fine Brunel overall roof, Falmouth had this unusual canopy over the main platform. With its tightly curved corrugated iron roof it was unlike any other structure within Cornwall; in fact, it was almost certainly unique on the entire GWR system. The cranes of the docks are in the background, but the wagons visible are in the station yard; the line to the quay descended steeply from adjacent to the station approaches.

Two North British Type '2's, No's D6308 and D6315, arriving at Falmouth with the 07.30 from Paddington on a summer Saturday in August 1968. The train would have been worked by a 'Warship' or 'Western' as far as Plymouth. The station has already been severely rationalised, cut back to a run-round loop beyond the single platform (behind the coaches) shown here. The station was closed in 1970 and a new halt built half a mile back up the line, but the old station re-opened in 1975 taking the name of Falmouth Docks, the halt becoming Falmouth Town. The line to the docks off the run round loop also survived but is currently mothballed.

Helston

The 8¾ mile branch to Helston, Britain's most southerly station, was opened in 1877. The GWR operated its first bus service, from Helston to The Lizard, in August 1903 using two ex-Lynton & Barnstaple Railway Milnes Daimler buses. The branch was closed to passengers on 5th November 1962, the first closure of a Cornish branch line to passengers since 1929. In the mid-1950s, the branch was worked by three '45xx' 2-6-2Ts supplied by Penzance Shed, one of which stabled overnight at Helston. Two of the engines were used on freight duties, with the third handling all of the passenger trains and also shunting between its journeys. The Helston Branch was closed to freight in 1964, and the track lifted in 1965, with the track bed sold off to private owners. However, a preservation group was formed in 2002 and after seven years' clearance work one mile of track has been re-laid with a long-term aim to restore the section between Nancegollan and Helston. Passenger services started in December 2011 with a Ruston diesel shunter and a BR Brake Van.

Penzance's '45xx' No. 4566 seems to crop up in many photographs of Cornish branch lines. It was working a freight on the Helston Branch at Praze on 22nd September 1961 but had not stopped to top-up its tanks at the characteristic Great Western conical water tower. No. 4566 moved to Laira in October and after withdrawal in April 1962 it was sent to Barry Docks scrapyard which has enabled it to survive into preservation at the Severn Valley Railway.

North British Type '2' No. D6312 calls at Praze with a train for Helston around 1962. This is another example of a 'one-for-one' replacement of steam; it could have been a '45xx' on the 'B-set' shuffling backward and forwards between Helston and Gwinear Road. Remarkably, as shown here on the extreme left, Praze retained its GWR pre-grouping blue enamel station sign until closure – hopefully someone saved it for posterity.

Another Penzance 'Small Prairie', No. 4570 at Nancegollan, the only passing point on the branch, with the usual two-coach Helston Branch train on 13th August 1959. In the late 1930s, the Great Western Railway made a significant investment in new goods facilities at Nancegollan to cater for the extensive agricultural traffic generated in the area, Helston having been rejected because of the limited land available for expansion there.

Whilst heading for Helston the driver of No. D6312 looks back at Nancegollan to see there are two doors still open and the guard is seemingly distracted. Even with only 1,100bhp, the acceleration would be good with just two coaches, but the branch was short and therefore it was not easy to make up lost time.

No. 4563 at Truthall Halt on 29th May 1961 with a freight. The halt was opened in 1905 to serve nearby Truthall Manor and the hamlet of Trannack, and consisted of a single platform built from wooden sleepers with a corrugated iron pagoda shelter.

No. 4563 at a deserted Helston terminus in the late-1950s. It still has a pre-World War One enamel (blue on white) 'Station Master' sign, visible behind the more modern 'Gentlemen' sign.

CHAPTER 5 - WESTERN REGION CORNISH BRANCH LINES

Another view of No. 4563, showing the experimental 'Helston' sign on the lamp post – this was the only station where these were used. A second 2-6-2T is just visible standing on the site of the carriage shed, which was demolished in 1958, in the background beyond the goods shed. The goods traffic is busier than the passenger business on this day, an indication why two of the three engines working the branch were usually occupied on freight work.

One of the last five of the original '45xx' engines, No. 4570 after arrival at Helston. It spent almost thirty years in Cornwall, from May 1935 until July 1962, punctuated only by a two month spell at Newton Abbot in early 1937.

St. Ives

The short, 4¼ miles long branch from St. Erth to St. Ives was opened in 1877, the last broad gauge line to be constructed, and was converted to standard gauge in 1892. It was scheduled for closure under the Beeching Plan and was mentioned in the 1963 Flanders and Swann 'Slow Train' song about the closures, but fortunately was reprieved by the Minister of Transport. The track layout at St. Ives was simplified in late 1963 after the freight service ceased, and the engine and goods sheds were demolished. The distinctive stone-built station building on its curved platform was closed in May 1971 and a new, straight, platform opened on the site of the goods shed, with the space created used to provide a car park.

Left: The '45xx' tanks worked almost all the traffic on the St. Ives Branch for around thirty years from the early 1930s onwards, taking over from the smaller-wheeled '44xx' Class which had been predominant since their introduction in 1906; two engines were in use on weekdays. Penzance Shed's No. 4570 is at Carbis Bay in the 1950s.

Below: Another 'Small Prairie' from Penzance, No. 4564 near Carbis Bay on 29th May 1961. The regular passenger service on the line significantly increased on summer Saturdays with twenty-one trains to St. Ives and seventeen to St. Erth in 1959, with two through workings from Paddington.

CHAPTER 5 - WESTERN REGION CORNISH BRANCH LINES

The replacement for the original stone built Carbis Bay station in all its glory! Based on the registration number of the Austin 2200 in the foreground this picture dates from the early 1970s. The marketing of rail services was far from slick at this time: the chalked board on the left urges potential passengers to 'Ask for a Cornish seaside bargain leaflet:- Trips to Falmouth, Looe and Newquay for £1 Adults and 50p Children over 3 yrs and under 14 yrs' – what happened to children over 14 is not stated! The board on the right was advertising daily excursions to Plymouth for £1.55.

The line passes through some spectacular scenery as shown by No. 4564 running almost on the cliff edge of St. Ives Bay on 29th May 1961.

The terminus at St. Ives was built on a curved embankment above Porthminster Beach. It featured a stone goods shed, in the centre of the photograph, and a small engine shed, just visible on the left, to hold the branch locomotive overnight. The inevitable '45xx' departs for St. Erth on 7th August 1957.
HC Casserley

No. 4566 is running around its train in September 1955 as a large number of holidaymakers make their way along the platform towards the ticket barrier.

On Wednesday 5th June 1957, still working on the branch, No. 4566 has run around its train and is ready to depart with the 11.45am to St. Erth. Station staff are cleaning the spare carriages parked in the bay. The weekday service on the branch used two pairs of 'B-sets' and was allowed fifteen minutes for the four-mile journey.

No. 4566, pictured on 14th August 1958, was a regular on the line and it can still be seen today on the Severn Valley Railway, having been rescued from Woodham Brothers' scrapyard in 1970. No. 4566 has brought in a five coach train with three additional vehicles coupled in front of the usual 'B-set'. The '45xx' in the distance will take the train back to St. Erth since No. 4566 has stopped on the turnout for the run-round loop.

The stone-built engine shed at St. Ives was 40ft long and held a single '45xx'; it had an inspection pit inside and another outside. It was in operation until September 1961, although steam engines still worked occasional trains until the following year. The water tank held 6,850 gallons, was 20ft × 11ft × 5ft high and was mounted on 14in. deep ornate lattice girders supported on columns on top of a 6ft high stone-built coaling stage. The engine shed siding was taken out of use in September 1963.

No. 4566 was probably working to St. Ives prior to returning coupled to No. 4564 as shown in the photograph opposite. The '45xx' tanks began to be replaced by 'D6300' Type '2's from August 1961, with steam officially ending on 9th September, although at first they shared the workings, before complete dieselisation came the following year.

A view towards the buffer stops showing the small bay in which the limited goods traffic was parked waiting to be taken back to St. Erth. The goods yard was on the left just outside the frame of this picture and was operational until 1963. No. 4564 will work back to St. Erth with No. 4566.

CHAPTER 5 - WESTERN REGION CORNISH BRANCH LINES

No. 4564 is back-to-back with classmate No. 4566 in the summer of 1961, with the two 2-6-2Ts hauling two pairs of 'B-sets'. The branch had two sets of these 1930s built Diagram E140 61ft 2in. coaches. The first of these started on the 6.15am from St. Ives, running eleven return trips to St. Erth, and the second set started from St. Erth at 5.15pm, working the evening services. They were worked together for the 5.37pm from St. Ives, as shown in this picture, then ran independently as the 6.05pm and 6.37pm trains from St. Erth, after which the second set worked the remainder of the day's services. No. 4564 was in Cornwall for only four years, arriving at St. Blazey in February 1959 and moving to Penzance two months' later; it moved north to Gloucester in September 1963.

Once again No. 4566 is working the passenger service and has run round its train, the crew have not yet positioned the lamps which will have to be done before departing for St Erth.

The branch passenger service was taken over by diesels in September 1961; initially the service was worked by 'D6300' Type '2's and 'B-sets', but these were soon replaced by DMUs. In this 1966 picture the original stone station building is still extant although it was demolished soon after. A new 'Park and Ride' station was opened in 1978 at Lelant and this generated substantial traffic with over twenty return workings each day as the town centre of St. Ives became increasingly congested and almost impassable for cars during the summer months.